On Time,
Change, History,
and Conversion

READING AUGUSTINE

Series Editor:

Miles Hollingworth

Reading Augustine offers personal and close readings of St. Augustine of Hippo from leading philosophers and religious scholars. Its aim is to make clear Augustine's importance to contemporary thought and to present Augustine not only or primarily as a pre-eminent Christian thinker but as a philosophical, spiritual, literary, and intellectual icon of the West.

On Time, Change, History, and Conversion

Sean Hannan

BLOOMSBURY ACADEMIC

NEW YORK • LONDON • OXFORD • NEW DELHI • SYDNEY

BLOOMSBURY ACADEMIC
Bloomsbury Publishing Inc
1385 Broadway, New York, NY 10018, USA
50 Bedford Square, London, WC1B 3DP, UK

BLOOMSBURY, BLOOMSBURY ACADEMIC and the Diana logo are
trademarks of Bloomsbury Publishing Plc

First published in the United States of America 2020

Cover design: Terry Woodley
Cover image © Jule McKee, Getty

A catalogue record for this book is available from the British Library.

A catalog record for this book is available from the Library of Congress.

ISBN: HB: 978-1-5013-5647-6
       PB: 978-1-5013-5646-9
       ePDF: 978-1-5013-5650-6
       ePUB: 978-1-5013-5648-3

Typeset by Integra Software Services Pvt. Ltd.

To find out more about our authors and books visit www.bloomsbury.com
and sign up for our newsletters.

For Joshua Casteel

CONTENTS

ABBREVIATIONS

The following abbreviations will be used when referring to Augustine's writings. For CD, CF, CR, and DP, the translations will be my own. For DG and HJ, I have relied upon translations prepared by others.

CD *De Civitate Dei*. CCSL 47–48. Ed. B. Dombart and A. Kalb. Turnhout: Brepols, 1955.

CF *Confessiones*. CCSL 27. Ed. Luc Verheijen. Turnhout: Brepols, 1981.

CR *De Catechizandis Rudibus*. CCSL 46. Ed. J.-B. Bauer. Turnhout: Brepols, 1969.

DG *Literal Meaning of Genesis* [*De Genesi ad Litteram*]. Trans. Edmund Hill, O.P. Hyde Park, NY: New City, 2002.

DP *De Dono Perseverantiae*. Patrologia Latina XLV, 933–1034. Paris: Migne, 1865.

HJ *Homilies on 1 John*. In *Later Works*. Trans. John Burnaby. Philadelphia: Westminster, 1955.

Introduction

In its April 25, 2011 issue, the *New Yorker* profiled David Eagleman, a neuroscientist researching time-perception in human subjects (Bilger 2011). When he was a child, Eagleman fell almost to his death from a construction site. As he was plummeting, he felt as though time were slowing down. He could perceive every detail around him, from the grains of the wood to the reddishness of the bricks below, all within what could only have been a matter of milliseconds. As the moment of death approached, temporality contracted for him while his time-consciousness expanded. The flow of time shrunk to an instantaneous now, enabling his conscious experience to linger in that moment, at least until he hit the ground and lost consciousness entirely. Motivated by this childhood trauma, Eagleman devised an experiment in which his subjects toppled off of a high ledge with chronometers strapped to their wrists. These chronometers measured time at a speed normally illegible to the human eye. The experiment aimed to determine whether the death-defying leap would cause time-consciousness to slow down enough that the subject could read the rapidly changing numbers. Eagleman's experiment failed, albeit fruitfully. Human subjects could not read the chronometer, even as they fell to their near-deaths. Time failed to contract reliably into the present moment.

One conclusion to be drawn from Eagleman's experiment is that its initial assumptions about the subjective nature of temporality were flawed. In retrospect, it may feel as though we linger in certain moments longer than others, but the hard reality of time still tends to hit us all with the same dull thud. Rather than a heterogeneous sequence of meaningful events, time instead strikes us as a homogeneous line, its empty objectivity bludgeoning us into submission as we are dragged toward our inevitable deaths. This picture of time lacks the romanticism of Eagleman's original view, with its painterly sensibility about the indelibility of life-altering moments. Yet the objective portrait arguably remains the truer account. It is also the depiction that matches best the account of temporality found in the works of Augustine.

For Augustine, time is all too real. It conditions every aspect of our lives, from the personal experience of everyday life to the world-historical plane of sociopolitical transformation. In each case, our presumption to certainty is unsettled by philosophical questions. What is the relationship between temporal experience and time itself? What takes pride of place between the past, the present, and the future? Should I live in the moment or await the end to come? The most crucial question concerns the puzzle that we turn out to be for ourselves. "I have become a great question to myself," as Augustine put it (CF 4.4.9).[1] This question of the self is asked but never really answered in time. A proper solution must await the dissolution of time in eternity.

These problems orbiting around time's impenetrable core come to a head whenever we reflect upon moments of apparent transformation. For Eagleman, this role was played by the near-death experience, a world-reshaping event that overshadows the mundane passages of our quotidian existence. For Augustine, these moments of transformation came in many shapes and sizes. On the level of the individual person, they are called conversions; on the level of political history, they are called revolutions; on the level of cosmic history, they are epoch-shifting events. Augustine treats all of these in his works. The overarching theme shared by each treatment is the idea that the objective flow of time continues to disrupt our dream that there are discernible moments which actively reshape our temporal lives as we live through them. Instead, we always find ourselves pulled along into the future by time's current, grasping feebly backward into the past as we retroactively attempt to reconstruct what just happened. Sometimes, we get it wrong, just as Eagleman did when he assumed that his own childhood memory would bear scientific fruit.

Augustine was not the first to be troubled by time, of course. Near the dawn of the fifth century, when he sat down and tried to figure out time in *Confessions* 11, the paradoxes he stumbled upon already had a history. Plotinus, a third-century philosopher trained in Alexandria, is usually taken to be the figure who most anticipates Augustine on questions of time. That reputation is earned by the fact that Plotinus devoted a whole treatise in his *Enneads* to time and eternity. Nevertheless, Plotinus' goal there is to spin a myth about psyche's descent from the static realm of mind or *nous*. Psyche is here taken as temporal, discursive thought, whereas mind is the locus of the timeless thought of truth. The distinction drawn here between the temporal and the timeless will go on to inform Augustine's account of time and eternity. What Plotinus lacks, however, is an obsessive concern with the problem of the present time and the possibility of living through transformative moments in the present. Insofar as that is the case, Augustine's approach is more reminiscent of earlier Greek engagements with temporality. His concern about the status of the present, for example, harkens backs to the Eleatic puzzles posed by Plato in the *Parmenides*, where we find both Zeno's paradox and some confusion regarding the possibility of sudden transformation. In the fourth book of Aristotle's *Physics*, meanwhile, similar questions are raised about the status of the now as a moment on the timeline. The Peripatetic method reduces the now to a retroactively posited limit, which is more useful for mathematical measurement than for lived experience.

Despite these philosophical parallels, Augustine was not primarily concerned with decoding Platonic dialogues or unpacking Aristotelian treatises. More authoritative than the *Timaeus* or the *Physics* were those books he had come to recognize as divine Scripture. For him, thinking about time was not idle speculation, but exegesis. *Confessions* 11 is the first in a three-book interpretation of the beginning of Genesis. It is the beginning of an essay on creation. Since Augustine seldom read any passage of Scripture in isolation, it is no surprise that those final books of the *Confessions* connect Genesis to the epistles of Paul. In Paul's letters, Augustine found a new sense of temporality which mapped only imperfectly onto the theories of the Platonists or the Aristotelians. This new kind of temporality was shaped by Paul's messianic and eschatological message. What mattered for Paul was what it felt like to live in the time between the messiah's death and his return. A Pauline sense of being stretched apart between crucial occasions in history embedded itself at the heart of Augustine's account of temporal experience.

For Plato, then, the question of time had taken the shape of a paradox concerning how one thing is able to change into another within one present moment. For Aristotle, it became a question of number and measure. In Paul's letters, meanwhile, the present became distorted or stretched out between two turning points in salvation history: the first and second arrivals of the messiah. Augustine's troubles with time arise out of a strange mixture of those three facets of the problem of the present. With Plato, Augustine shares some confusion about how people could possibly change in an instant. Like Aristotle, he is skeptical that time itself is made up of real chunks called "nows." And, in the spirit of Paul, whose writings he knew far better than those of any Greek philosopher, Augustine kept alive the notion that existence is defined as much by moments missed as by events experienced. By moving beyond the confines of the present, his writings expressed what it is like to live and change in time, stretched apart as we are between the past and the future. Once Augustine dethroned the present from its privileged position at the core of time, his emphasis on the necessity of retrospective cognition (commonly called memory) emerged as a consequence. Augustinian temporality, in other words, has little to do with living in the now and much to do with a sense that we are somehow running late, unable to catch up to the present moment. This is why our temporal experience is best defined in terms of memory, retrospection, and, in a word, belatedness.

1

The Reality of Time

Between Idealism and Materialism

Introduction

In a dialogue published in 2017, the object-oriented ontologist Graham Harman and the neo-materialist Manuel DeLanda cordially clarified the differences between their respective approaches to philosophy. Both are opposed to what they see as widespread acceptance of naïve idealism among thinkers in the contemporary continental tradition. For DeLanda, a robust materialism, rooted in the "projectiles" and "shrapnel" of the late modern battlefield, offers the best rejoinder to these anti-realists. Harman, meanwhile, rejects materialism in favor of a realism rooted in all objects, regardless of the question of their materiality or immateriality (DeLanda and Harman 2017: 3). As the dialogue progresses, it turns out that a number of divergences between these two approaches can be dissolved simply by translating the terminology of object-oriented ontology into that of neo-materialism and vice versa. Even so, real differences do remain. The most divisive dispute emerges only later in the discussion, when Harman and DeLanda discover that they disagree about whether objective existence can be ascribed to time itself.

Setting aside the merits of the anti-idealism espoused by Harman and DeLanda, it must be admitted that, at least in the philosophy of time, even the analytic tradition continues to wrestle with idealism. This is in part due to the long shadow cast by the British idealist J. M. E. McTaggart's 1908 essay "The Unreality of Time," the meaning of which continues to be debated. McTaggart, for his part, thought he was clarifying matters by distinguishing between the A-Series (temporal sequence considered in terms of past, present, and future) and the B-Series (temporal sequence considered merely in terms of earlier and later). If both series could be proven to be products of the mind rather than properties of a mind-independent time, then the idealist conclusion would follow: time is unreal. It is this idealizing approach that the new wave of realists seeks to overcome. The question of time, in their view, should be answered not with logical subtleties, but with inescapable realities.

Looking further into the past, we can see that the disagreement between Harman and DeLanda brings us back beyond nineteenth-century British idealism, even to the writings of a fourth-century North African bishop. In *Confessions* 11, Augustine tackled the problem of time's being from a perspective informed not just by his Christianity, but also by the developed Platonism he had encountered in the teachings of Plotinus. His response to the paradoxes of temporality would nonetheless prove distinctive. While some interpreters of Augustine have positioned him as a subjectivist or an idealist with regard to time, a close reading of Augustine's account reveals that he attributes objective reality to the force of time. His central discovery is that time is a distensive force which stretches many things, including the human soul, apart. By rereading Augustine in light of the new realisms of Harman and DeLanda, perhaps we can better appreciate the objective dimensions of his argument, as well as what it might have to offer to contemporary debates about temporality.

Temporal Materialisms

The disagreement between Harman and DeLanda emerges as they confront the confusion caused by their jargon. In order to determine whether or not they agree, the two authors first have to get straight what their words actually mean. Nowhere is this clearer than in the matter of time.

For DeLanda, time is simply time. It is the objective time measured by clocks. It is duration in the plainest sense. It is the unidirectional arrow of time, equally compatible with the physical world of entropy and the martial world of soldiers torn apart by shrapnel, never again brought back to life. For Harman, temporality is not so straightforward. His system ascribes new meaning to the word "time," which must be understood in light of his fourfold division of the modes of tension that can obtain between objects and their qualities. The system breaks down into four kinds of tension (and here comes the jargon): tension between sensual objects and sensual qualities; tension between real objects and sensual qualities; tension between real objects and real qualities; and tension between sensual objects and real qualities. Each mode of tension corresponds to one of four load-bearing terms: time (SO-SQ), space (RO-SQ), essence (RO-RQ), and eidos (SO-RQ). Harman's time, following this model, has to do with relations between sensual objects and sensual qualities. It is this association of temporality with the sensual that alarms DeLanda, who suspects it leads down a slippery slope to subjectivism. "Is this real time, as measured by clocks," asks DeLanda (2017: 122), "or subjectively experienced time?"

Harman's reply initially lends credence to DeLanda's worries. "Here I'm speaking about the lived time of experience," says Harman (2017: 122), adding that "it is the relative endurance of sensual objects amidst a constant shift of adumbrations." The subjective air of this response risks confusing the situation. "Are you not a realist with respect to time?" prods DeLanda (2017: 122). If time is reduced to a function of the sensual, there may be no room left for the objective duration which seems necessary for any realism worth the name. Harman, of course, disagrees. For him, reducing time to the sensual need not undermine the possibility of physical change, entropy, or any of the objective processes which DeLanda means to protect. All of these, Harman implies, can be categorized under his concept of "space," which deals with the tension between real objects and sensual qualities, and is therefore capable of preserving succession, alteration, and so on. "What you're calling real time as measured by a clock belongs, for me, to space," says Harman (2017: 122), "since it has to do with changes in real objects rather than just sensual experience." Time, meanwhile, remains framed in terms of a living present. Elsewhere, Harman (2011: 176) writes of the centrality of presentism in object-oriented ontology:

According to the object-oriented model, only the present exists: only objects with their qualities, locked into whatever their duels of the moment might be. In that sense, times seem to be illusory, though not for the usual reason that time is just a fourth spatial dimension always already present from the start. Instead time does not exist simply because only the present ever exists.

The living present of sensual time reminds many readers of subjective interpretations of temporality. Some have even criticized Harman as a philosopher of stasis (Shaviro 2011; Gratton 2013). From DeLanda's point of view, it seems Harman stumbled into a form of subjectivism at the heart of his objective thinking, which in turn led him to rule objective temporality out of his analysis.

Even in earlier works like *Guerrilla Metaphysics*, Harman (2005: 248–53) happily conceded he harboured doubts about time as an objective dimension of the cosmos. Here Harman (2017: 124) is more emphatic: "If we consider time as belonging to the real itself, then I guess I'm *not* a realist about time." Yet, despite DeLanda's protests, Harman is not committing himself to subjectivism. As becomes clearer near the end of the dialogue, Harman (2017: 131) finds his refuge in the proposition both authors agree to denote as R7: "The relation of the human subject with the world is not a privileged relation for philosophy." What R7 allows Harman to do, in the matter of temporality, is preserve the idea of the living present by liberating it from the human subject and projecting it out onto everything that exists. This is to mobilize anthropomorphism in order to overcome anthropocentrism, he suggests. The living present is not just for subjects perceiving phenomena; the living present is the key to the structure of time itself.

As the dialogue ends, DeLanda magnanimously grants most of his interlocutor's claims. He concedes that proposition R7 helps Harman escape the accusation of subjectivism about time. Nevertheless, he remains suspicious that Harman's temporality is insufficiently objective. The concern seems to be no longer that this account of time privileges human experience, but rather that material changes taking place in the real world (as DeLanda sees it) demand a temporality closer to objective duration than any "living present" model could allow. And so we arrive at a clarified but still meaningful divergence. Harman offers us a new vantage point on time, which suits his system but demands we shift features long associated with time (e.g., succession) into the category of space. DeLanda, meanwhile, argues for the necessity of taking time as real duration, although he is unable to undermine Harman's own arguments to the contrary. These are not the only two available positions, however. As we turn to Augustine, we will see that it is possible to hold simultaneously to an objective account of time and a non-presentist account of temporal duration. Harman's centering of objects is already provocative, but more provocative still would be an account of objective temporality that found itself rooted in the death of the living present.

Time as *Distentio*

The context for Augustine's account of an objective, non-presentist temporality is his exegesis of Genesis in *Confessions* 11–13. Already with the words "in the beginning," he spies potential confusion. Was this the beginning of time or the beginning of the universe in time? And what is time anyway? Given the importance of time to our workaday existence, it seems the answer should be obvious, though it is not. It feels like we understand time, but, when pressed, we fail to express anything close to a compelling description (CF 11.14.17). Nevertheless, some things have passed away; others are still to come. This arising and passing occur in time. They could also be correlated to the linguistic tenses of past and future. And yet the past and future pose more problems than they solve, since they deal with what is not (either what has passed away or what has yet to arrive) rather than what is. What then about the present? If present time truly is, in a way that past and future are not, must this mean that the present is beyond arising or passing away? Is it pure presence without any vulnerability to time's passage? If so, the present would be eternity, says Augustine (CF 11.14.17):

> In what way, then, "are" those two times, past and future, when the past "is" no longer and the future "is" not yet? The present, moreover, if it were always present and did not pass away into the past, would no longer be time, but eternity. In order that there be time, then, the present is created for this reason: in order to pass over into the past. How, then, can we also say that this

present "is," whose cause for being is that it will not be? That is to say: is it that we cannot say in truth that time "is," unless because it tends to not-be?[1]

Arising and passing away reveal to us that there is nothing eternal about our world. For Augustine, eternity amounts to timelessness, and so to posit the present as a quasi-eternity within time would be incoherent and potentially blasphemous (since eternity is proper to God). Our present time, if there is one, would always be in the process of passing away. The present too has become a problem for Augustine.

Yet even if he has stumbled out of the gate in his search for time's definition, Augustine had to admit that we are always talking about the measurement of time. Some times appear to be short; others strike us as long. But when we speak of short or long times, we are treating time-spans as if they were entities. We are taking "a time" to be long or short. As van Dusen (2014) has argued, Augustine's language brings us face to face with the flexibility of the Latin *tempus*, not unlike the English "time." Both terms could mean: (1) time itself, as the pure passage that we later cut up into tenses of past, present, and future; or (2) a time-span within that overall passage, which we mark out and measure as long or short. Such spans can be as short as a line from a hymn or as long as the circuit of a star. In cases like these, we are talking not about time proper, but rather about our own cognitive measurements of delineated spans of time. Augustine dubs these *morae* or delays (CF 11.15.19). These spans or delays can only be measured as long or short by way of our memories.

If we look for something like length or shortness in time itself, we come up short. It is only in the soul's psychological experience of time that we find such measurements. The soul measures these magnitudes neither as solely past nor as solely future, but rather as a kind of duration through which we seem to live in the present. After pointing his readers to the present as the only conceivable site of duration, however, Augustine turns the tables on us, intensifying his critique of the present. He starts by calling attention to the relativism involved in our talk about present spans of time. The present year or month or day or hour, which we might be tempted to call long, can always be whittled down into smaller pasts and futures. Within each minute there are always some seconds that are past and others to come. Even one second harbours within itself ever-more-microscopic past and future spans (CF 11.15.20):

> Look at how the present time, which we found to be the only thing that ought to be called "long," has with difficulty been reduced to the space of one day. But let us break it apart even further. One day is not present as a whole. It is filled out with all twenty-four daytime and night-time hours. The first hour holds the rest as "going-to-be," the last as "having-passed-away," and, of course, one of the middle hours would hold those before itself to be past and those after itself to be future. Even an hour itself passes by little bits which flee away. Whatever part of it has flown away is past; whatever remains for it is future.[2]

If we want to be rigorous about our definition of the present, then we must not allow ourselves lazy locutions that treat as present that which is still divisible into past and future. Augustine draws from this the following consequence (CF 11.15.20):

> If we conceive of something temporal which could no longer be divided into little parts of movements: that alone is what could be called "present." And yet it flies immediately from future to past, so that it is stretched out by not even the smallest pause. For if it is stretched out, it is divided between past and future. But the present has no span.[3]

If the present is without pause or quasi-spatial extent, it cannot have duration of either the long or short variety. This is in keeping with what Augustine said earlier about the three temporal tenses all collapsing into an abyss of non-being.

Next, however, Augustine reminds us that we nevertheless do "experience intervals of time and compare them with one another"[4] (CF 11.16.21). Time-spans are still a part of temporal experience, even though they are not a part of time. It cannot be denied that people never stop talking about past and future things. But Augustine is quick to point out that even when we speak of past or future things as present, we are talking about images of what was or will be, not the things themselves. Past things are mediated to us by images in our memory, future things by images of what we expect or await. Augustine is preparing to work these aspects of the soul into a triadic structure of temporal experience. This is what is usually called his threefold present (CF 11.20.26):

> Neither future nor past things are, and it is not correct to say: "there are three times—past, present, and future." Rather, it would perhaps be more correct to say: "there are three times— the present time concerning what has passed away; the present time concerning what is 'there;' and the present time concerning what will be." These three somethings are in the living soul. I do not see them anywhere else. The present time having to do with past things is memory. The present time having to do with present things is awareness. The present time having to do with future things is expectation.[5]

The triad of tenses long plaguing Augustine is revealed for what it really is: a categorization of temporal experience, not of time. The scheme of past, present, and future has failed to give us a coherent way of speaking about time proper.

By saying that past, present, and future really pertain only to the ongoing experience of the soul, however, Augustine is not saying that time is identical to the soul. Time was created along with the universe; its passage continues according to God's wisdom. Nor is he saying that there is no distinction between what has yet to arise and what has already passed away. The flux of creation does not collapse into a quasi-eternity made possible by the soul's threefold present. On the contrary, Augustine undermines our tensed way of talking about time, which lasts down through McTaggart's A-Series. This means that the present, just like the past and future, lacks the substance necessary to support our sense that we are measuring temporal duration as it happens. As Augustine writes (CF 11.21.27):

> And yet how do we measure the present time, when it has no span? We measure as it passes by. But when it has passed by, it is not measured. For what could be measured would not be. But where is time passing "from," "through," or "to" as we measure it? Where is it coming from if not the future? What is it passing through if not the present? What is it passing over to if not the

past? Time passes, then, from what is not yet, through what lacks any span, and into what no longer is. But what do we measure if not some span of time?[6]

Taken naïvely, the triad of memory, awareness, and expectation led us to hope that we would have access to past and future time-spans by way of the present. Sadly, however, this triad applies only to time-consciousness, not to time itself. The present still has no span.

Augustine has stumbled upon a tangled riddle at the heart of seemingly obvious matters. Praying for the strength to face the challenges posed by time, he acknowledges that others failed before him, referring most harshly to those who define "the times" as the motion of heavenly bodies (CF 11.23.29). Of course, he admits that days and seasons are measured by way of the sun and stars. But he refuses to conclude from this that time is reducible to motion. While motion occurs in time, time is something other than the movements we refer to as we chop time up into measurable spans. Augustine (CF 11.23.30) goes on to clarify what he is after: "I want to know the force and nature of time. I am talking about the time by which we measure the motion of bodies and say that one motion is, for example, twice as long as some other motion."[7] Invoking Josh. 10, in which the sun stands still while time runs on, Augustine declares his interest not so much in the astronomical calendar as in time simpliciter. This distinction suggests that his discussions of measurement and experience were only means to the end of approaching the force and nature of time. If we too want to understand this force and nature, we must be careful to avoid mistaking our own temporal selves for time itself.

The fact that time is not reducible to moments, movements, or measurements need not mean it escapes description entirely. "I see," confesses Augustine (CF 11.23.30), "that time is some kind of stretching-out [*distentio*]. But do I see it? Or do I only seem to myself to be seeing it?" He cannot tell if he is looking at time or conjuring up an image of time based on temporal experience. "It has become clear to me," he writes (CF 11.26.33), "that time is nothing other than a stretching-apart. But I do not know what thing is being stretched apart, if it is not, strangely, the soul itself."[8] This is how we get from *distentio*, the force and nature of time, to *distentio animi*, the application of that force to the *animus* or soul. We should not make the mistake of reading this *animi* as a subjective or possessive genitive, in which case *distentio* would belong to the soul. To do so would be to commit a hasty misreading shared by philosophical tourists like Bertrand Russell (1948: 212) and serious readers of Augustine like Etienne Gilson (1960: 189–96), R.A. Markus (1967: 402–5), and Richard Sorabji (1983: 29–30). It is also common in the recent specialist literature (Mendelson 2000; Humphries 2009; Strozynski 2009). Fortunately, the misreading is not universal (Jordan 1955; Lacey 1968; Gundersdorf von Jess 1972; Ross 1991; Quinn 1992). Building on the work of those who have uncovered an objective account of time in *Confessions* 11, we can say that Augustine's description of *distentio* or "stretching apart" is not primarily the achievement of any soul. It is instead the way the soul must live, since it lives in time. *Distentio animi* is better read as an objective genitive. *Distentio* happens. It is the force and nature of time. The thing it happens to is the soul, which is the object of this transitive force.

If *distentio* were the soul's subjective achievement, this would contradict Augustine's earlier demonstrations on a number of fronts. Above all, it would be difficult to rectify with his affirmation that time and the universe were created simultaneously, as his reading of Genesis 1 suggests. If time is reducible to a soul's expansion, would we not need some soul whose expansion would constitute the time of the universe? And would not the multiplicity of human souls, each making time by accomplishing *distentio*, lead to a multiplication of times throughout the world? Only with great effort can such ideas be forced upon Augustine, leading to the imposition of extrinsic ideas like a world-soul or the anteriority of angelic consciousness, serving as the Christian proxy for a world-soul (Teske 1983, 1996; Rogers 1994, 1996). Neither of these possibilities is discussed in *Confessions* 11. To its detriment, a subjectivist reading of Augustine must also presume a stable atom of time, from which the soul could initiate the expansion of its own presence. But that is precisely what *Confessions* 11 denies. Augustine's *distentio* is consonant with his critique of the present, which has in no way been overcome here. Taking *distentio animi* as an objective genitive, meanwhile, fits plausibly with Augustine's claims concerning the non-being of past, present, and future.

Returning to the problem of measurement, Augustine next clarifies that we can only measure time-spans once their duration has ended. We cannot, for example, say how long a sound lasted until it lasts no longer (CF 11.27.34). Only afterward can we posit an interval extended between two points. This does not mean we measure past times, since those time-spans are gone. Rather, we measure impressions in our memory (CF 11.27.36). Our access to time-spans is mediated by the delayed effect of affective memory. Augustine's example is the spoken syllable (CF 11.27.35):

> How could I measure the long [syllable] itself while it is present, when I can only measure what has ended? But its ending is a passing away. So what is it that I measure? Where is the brief syllable by which I measure the long? Where is the long one that I am measuring? Both have made a sound, flown away, passed away—they no longer are. Yet I measure them and I respond confidently (however much the stimulation of the senses can be trusted) that this one is twice as much as the other, that is, in its time-span. I can only do this because they have ended and passed away. And so I do not measure that which no longer is, but rather something which remains fixed in my memory.[9]

Aristotle made a similar point in *Physics* 4, arguing that spans of time could only be demarcated through limits later projected onto the temporal continuum by the mind. The now itself was just such a retroactive limit. Even though he probably never read the *Physics*, Augustine is making a quasi-Aristotelian move by emphasizing both the present's lack of a span and the retrospective nature of temporal measurement.

Memory, for Augustine, works in concert with awareness and expectation. Yet, given the necessity of retrospection, it bears the brunt of the labor when it comes to measuring spans of time. If we take all three facets of temporal experience into view, we witness them in a delicate interplay (CF 11.28.37):

> The soul awaits, attends, and remembers. What it awaits passes over into what it remembers by means of what it pays attention to. Who, then, would deny that things which are going to be are not yet? And yet already, in the soul, there is an awaiting for things that are going to be. And who would deny that things that have passed away no longer are? And yet still, in the soul, there

is a memory of past things. And again, who would deny that present time lacks any span, because it passes in a point? And yet attention, through which what there will be passes through to absence, endures.[10]

Faced with the non-being of the past and future, Augustine reduces our experience of the past and future to our experience of images of the past and future. The strangest thing is that affective mediation also conditions present experience. In light of time's nature, all the present can do is pass in a point. Lacking a span, it is nothing more than a potential distinction between past and future. It resembles an Aristotelian limit. With the point-like now abandoned, the soul continues to affectively attend to its fellow temporal beings, though such attention gains efficacy only in relation to memory and expectation. The idol of a self-sufficient present in time itself remains shattered.

Having addressed the problem of measurement by correlating the three tenses of time to the structure of temporal experience, Augustine takes a turn toward lamentation as his book draws to a close. His pretty picture of memory, awareness, and expectation has done little to heal the pain he feels under time's distensive force. He confesses:

Look at how my life is a stretching-apart [*distentio*]. Your right hand picked me up and brought me to my Lord, the human mediator. He mediates between you, who are One, and us, who are many. We are in many things and we pass through many things. And You brought me to Him, so that I might take hold of Him by whom I was already held, so that I might be gathered up from my aged days and chase after one thing, having forgotten all that has passed away—so that I might chase not after those things that are going to be and pass away, but after those things that are "before" ...[11]

The reference is to Philippians. In order to overcome the strain of time's *distentio*, Augustine needs something more than the threefold mechanism outlined above. He needs salvation. His reading of Paul told him this could only come from Christ, the Mediator between time and timelessness. In Paul's eschatological framework, Augustine glimpsed the possibility of a messianic resolution to the problem of temporality. His reflections on measurement, meanwhile, had merely raised deeper questions which were likely to stay unresolved until the end of time. And yet there remains a way out. Continuing the above passage, Augustine (CF 11.29.39) says he was brought to an awareness of the eternal God:

> ... so that I might be stretched out, not stretched apart; so that I might chase after that victory palm of the calling from above, not distractedly but intently. If I could win this palm, I would hear a voice of praise and contemplate your delight, which neither arrives nor passes away. Now, of course, my years are full of groans. You are my relief, Lord. You are eternal, my father. But I am ripped apart in times. I have no idea what their order is. My thoughts and the innermost guts of my soul will be torn to shreds by unstable differences until I flow into you, purified and melted down by the fire of your love.[12]

This passage is riddled with tensile terminology, although the forms of tension noted by Augustine are not the same as Harman's fourfold division. Augustine's goal is to be "stretched out" (*extentus*) without getting "stretched apart" (*distentus*). He sees a way out of the torment of *distentio* in Paul's message of salvational *extentio*, though the timing of this escape remains in question. A conversion of *distentio* into *extentio* seems improbable here and now. Paul's rhetoric of running a race governs this passage, introducing a third tension: *intentio*, which can be rendered as focus, intent, or (in keeping with the image of the contest) the extension of an athlete's limbs as they desperately attempt to cross the finish line. *Intentio* must be pursued against *distentio*, though this does not mean the pursuit has reached its target. It means the opposite. The human race is still being run. Augustine's years remain full of groans, as he is "ripped apart" in the varying time-spans of his unstable experience, ignorant of their proper order. In his guts, Augustine will be torn to shreds by time until some final, unimaginable melting-down into God's love. Only in this eschatological dissolution will Augustine be given the ability to convert *distentio* into *extentio*.

Temporal Experience as Belatedness

Augustine's critique of the present in *Confessions* 11 comes at a cost. The natural force of time as *distentio*, disrupting the present from within, makes it impossible for us to plant our feet in the middle of time's current. Instead, we are violently swept along. Never do we feel this pain more than during times of loss, but this need not mean that the pain is absent from us on seemingly happier occasions. *Distentio* leads not just to despair, but also to delusion. *Confessions* 4 provides an example of the former consequence; *Confessions* 10 delves deeper into the latter.

While all thirteen books of the *Confessions* are retrospective, the fourth makes retrospection an explicit problem. Memory is hard work, which means it only gets done well if God is helping us (CF 4.1.1). By the power of grace, Augustine is able to recall an unnamed friend in his hometown of Thagaste, whose death had left a scar on Augustine's soul. Both he and his friend had converted to Manichaeism, a movement devoted to the third-century prophet Mani and characterized by the ascesis of its elect or chosen ones, who were aided by the hearer or lay members. Mani revered Jesus, but positioned the saviour's role in the midst of a complex cosmology featuring multiple powers fighting either for the forces of light (good) or darkness (evil). Given their shared devotion to these teachings, Augustine was startled when his friend fell ill and, while unconscious, was baptized into a non-Manichaean branch of Christianity. Augustine took this as a farcical attempt by unscrupulous Christians to surreptitiously claim a new member. When his friend awoke, Augustine made some remarks to that effect which, to his great surprise, were met with scorn. Baptized unconsciously, the friend now consciously accepted his new devotion. Augustine could not understand the logic behind this. A few days later, his friend died, ruling out the possibility that the unconscious baptism had triggered miraculous healing (CF 4.4.8). All Augustine could feel was grief, attended by a sense of alienation from his own hometown. Everything he looked at could now only be seen in the dim light cast by memories of his friend. Strangest of all, he began to feel alienated even from himself. "I became a great question to myself," he said (CF 4.4.9).[13]

Confessions 4 is not just a book about grief. Augustine's loss invites him to face up to the fragility of his own self-awareness and the impermanence of things in general. If everything is going to perish, even beloved friends, then he must come to terms with this totalizing picture of loss. Anticipating *Confessions* 11, he casts his sorrow in terms of tearing, ripping, and pulling apart. He uncovers a wound within human experience that cuts deeper than any one instance of loss. "Every soul that is overcome by friendship with mortal things is miserable," declares Augustine (CF 4.6.11). "It is torn apart when it loses them. Then it feels the misery that was already there before it lost them." This misery of having a friend torn away calls us back to the prior misery of being torn apart from the beginning. The tearing-apart of loss is a manifestation of the stretching-apart of *distentio*. If we fail to appreciate this, we are doomed to pour our souls out onto the sand, holding on to what is impermanent as if it were going to last forever (CF 4.8.13).

Here, as in *Confessions* 11, Augustine moves between subjective observation and an objective exploration of the temporal universe. This accounts for his abrupt transition from the death of one friend to the impermanence of all things. The latter topic pushes him in the direction of cosmology, which might seem odd to readers expecting straight autobiography, though it makes sense in light of Augustine's association of time with the creation of the universe in Genesis. Although Augustine remains a realist about time, his approach to time's reality in *Confessions* 4 is aesthetic. He wants to know whether the temporal things we love are beautiful in themselves or only as part of an overarching sequence of arising and passing away. Augustine begins his cosmological reflection with an address to God:

> Wherever the human soul turns, it is bound to its pain, except when it is in You. Yet when it is bound to beautiful things, it is both outside of You and outside of itself. Still, those beautiful things would not "be" at all if they were not from You. These things arise and fall away. When they arise, it is as if they begin to be. They grow until they are mature. When they are mature, they grow old and are lost. Though not all grow old, all are lost.[14]

Augustine's response to personal death is to meditate on universal mortality. Sorrow drives him onward to speculation. He attempts a panoramic view of this world's beautiful things, which always slip through our fingers. But that is no defect. God made them; they are good. Their impermanence is not a mistake. It is simply their way of being. Augustine continues (CF 4.10.15):

> As they arise and stretch out towards being, it so happens that the more quickly they grow in order to be, the more they hurry up so that they are not. This is their limit. You gave them this much. They are parts of things, since they are not all together all at once. Instead, all things give place and take place, and thereby perform the whole, of which they are the parts.[15]

Augustine's cosmology is one of relational impermanence. It argues that withdrawal and coming forth is the way, limit, or measure (*modus*) of all things. All things fade away as they come to be, but in so doing they give their place to others. That is the limit of their finitude, which is not just destructive but generative. The performance of the whole sequence of the universe retains its beauty, even as the loss of each thing might cause grief. To steal a phrase from later in the *Confessions*, this is the beauty of the most beautiful order (CF 13.35).

The allure of this order is lost on humankind, for the most part, since we are attached to impermanent things as if they were permanent. We desire to keep them safe, but instead they rush by, as if they are already past before we reached out to grasp them. But God is not blind to this play of finitude, since the limits of all things are timelessly spoken in his Word (CF 4.10.15):

> These things go where they go, so that they are not. They tear the soul to pieces with sickening desires, since it wants to be and loves to rest in the things it loves. But in them there is no "where," since they do not stand still. Instead, they flee. And who could chase after them in incarnate experience? Incarnate experience is late, since it is incarnate experience. That is its limit. It is able to do certain things, since that is what it was made for. But it is not able to do this: that is, to hold things as they pass by, running from their obligatory beginning to their obligatory end. They were created through Your Word, and in Your Word they hear this: "From here up to here."[16]

The limits that the Word (also known as Christ) places on things by its ineffable speaking cannot be grasped by us as we live in the midst of said things. This is the case because we too are temporal. We have a *modus*, just like everything else in this beautiful, deadly order. That is why our experience is slow, late, or belated (*tardus*). The phrase he uses to describe incarnate experience is tinged with the hint of sin: it is the sense of the flesh. But its meaning is more than moral. It captures the limited way we engage with the temporal universe. "Whatever you sense through the flesh is only partial," writes Augustine (CF 4.11.17). "You do not even know the whole of which sensual things are just the parts, and yet still they delight you."[17] Moreover, he suggests that even if sin's censure were lifted, the insatiability of desire would drive us back into lust for permanence, rather than being satisfied with a consideration of the order of things. As Augustine writes (CF 4.11.17), here addressing humankind rather than God in the second person: "Even if your fleshly senses were suited for comprehending the whole, even if they had not received as their punishment a just limitation to a part of the whole, you would then want to go beyond whatever currently exists, just so that you could take even more pleasure in all things."[18] Our troubles with time are amplified by the consequences of Adam's fall, but they run deeper to the underlying structure of temporal experience. As it stands, humankind always arrives late to the scene of its own life. There was only one man who was ever on time. But to overcome belatedness, we would have to be as quick as Christ. "He was not late," conceded Augustine[19] (CF 4.12.19).

Since nobody should presume to have transcended time in the manner of Christ, we all need memory. *Confessions* 10 underlines the importance of memory as the facet of temporal experience which allows us to survive despite our belated way of being. For Augustine, *memoria* signifies more than memories. It is what lends the possibility of continuity to human life. Without it, we could not think at all. Even imaginative thought proceeds on the basis of images stored in memory's expansive estate (CF 10.8.12). *Memoria* further opens out onto the future, making anticipatory cognition possible (CF 10.8.14). Augustine also finds in memory the knowledge gained from mathematics and the liberal arts (CF 10.9.16; Miner 2007), the spectrum of feelings (CF 10.14.21), and, confusingly, the oblivion of forgetting (CF 10.16.24). However, the fact that memory is coextensive with human thinking does not mean we comprehend its power. All that we are is our memory, and yet we cannot grasp all that we are. "I myself do not grasp all that

I am," says Augustine (CF 10.8.15). "Is the soul then too narrow to contain itself?"[20] Just as in *Confessions* 4, we run up against our limits. By identifying ourselves with the mystery of memory, we are only posing new questions. As Augustine (CF 10.17.26) asks: "My God, what then am I? What nature am I?"[21]

In *Confessions* 4, Augustine's memory of his friend's death occasioned a reflection on the cosmic impermanence of all things as they arise and pass away. In *Confessions* 10, memory itself triggers in Augustine an awareness of the impermanence of his own thoughts, which also arise and pass away. His relationship to external and internal objects is equally belated. God alone is not late, whereas we can only ever be running late. All Augustine (CF 10.27.38) can say to God is: "I loved You too late, beauty so ancient, beauty so new. I loved You too late."[22] Yet even recognition of God's absolute punctuality is not enough to compensate for belatedness in this life. As Jean-Luc Marion (2012: 198) once suggested, "the difference between time and eternity can therefore be defined by a temporal belatedness." Much of the rest of *Confessions* 10 deals with how this belatedness becomes noticeable by way of our senses (which does not mean it leaves our souls unscathed). Augustine lists the five senses, noting what it is about each that tempts him most. Some of these accounts are more gripping than others. Augustine finds least tempting the realm of smell. Nevertheless, he lingers over this absence of olfactory temptation. He questions his own claim that no aroma tempts him, since it would presume he has a firm grasp on who he is (CF 10.32.48):

This is how I appear to myself, but perhaps I might be mistaken. There is this lamentable darkness in me. What I am capable of is concealed from me in this darkness, so that when my soul interrogates itself about its own strength, it cannot easily consider itself to be credible to itself. What lies within is entirely hidden, unless it is made manifest by experience. And in this life called total temptation, no one ought to be sure that he who can become better after being worse cannot also become worse after being better.[23]

Augustine's self-image cannot be trusted, since it lacks access to future experience. It is what Augustine is capable of doing in the future that scares him. The radical mutability of life cuts two ways.

It allows for progression, but also regression. For the time being, no one can trust themselves to diagnose their own condition. Only a completed life, the life of a dead person, could be liberated from the possibility of a future fall. The diagnosis awaits the autopsy.

Augustine next admits that his ear still serves as a passageway for sin. Long after his conversion and baptism, he remains preoccupied with beautiful sounds, especially hymns. Enjoying church music seems a mild crime, but to Augustine it was a sensual temptation like any other. During one service, for example, he was sitting before his congregation, listening soberly to the hymns being sung, when an intense delight flowed over him and took charge of his thoughts. He was no longer in control (CF 10.33.49):

> The delight of my flesh, to which a weak mind should not be given over, often deceives me. This happens when sense-experience does not follow upon reason, in such a way that it is patiently posterior. Instead, it merits admittance on account of its delightfulness, and it tries to run ahead and lead reason. In these kinds of things, I sin without feeling it. Only afterwards do I feel it.[24]

This is a strange feature of sin. The temptation is supposed to be sensual: Augustine is tempted by feeling. And yet he does not feel it. Or, rather, he does not feel it to be sin as he lives through the experience. Only in retrospect can he sense it to be something quite different from what he first felt. On account of this sensual belatedness, Augustine must rely on the mediation of memory in order to make sense of his own experiences.

In this same section on sonic temptation, Augustine repeats his claim about becoming a *quaestio* to himself. Still wavering on the issue of whether hymns are tools for sensual instruction or gateways to sensual destruction, he collapses into confused lamentation over what he himself even thinks (CF 10.33.50):

> You, my Lord God: hear me out! Look at me. See me. Have mercy on me and heal me. In your eyes, I have become a question to myself. And this itself is my weariness.[25]

When Augustine fails to settle his own feelings on something, it reminds him that he is still a question awaiting a future response.

Struggling to answer the question for himself only tires him out, leading to languid belatedness. Sticking closer to the meaning of *quaerere* as seeking, we could say that Augustine is in search of himself, trying to catch up and pin himself down as present: as this or that, as music-loving or music-reviling, as a good person or an evil person. And yet he cannot track himself down in time. Nothing has yet been able to resolve this question for him, as he confesses to God (CF 10.40.65): "In all these things that I run through and consult You about, I can find no safe place for my soul, except in You."[26] There is no rest from time, because time is real. *Distentio* is a force of nature. Scattered selves will only be gathered up at the eschatological harvest anticipated by Paul. Augustine's question must be deferred until the very end of time, since only a timeless God could answer it.

Conclusion

For Augustine, then, time is certainly not subjective in any naïve sense. Time is to be reduced neither to temporal experience nor to measurement. To that extent, Augustinian temporality remains an objective continuum. Yet we must be careful about framing time as an object for us, at least if we mean by that something we can grasp on our own terms. Directing our cognitive powers toward time as an object has the strange effect of decreasing our understanding of time. To paraphrase Augustine: time strikes us as familiar until we stop and think about it. Perhaps, like Harman's objects, time withdraws from our hubristic attempts to make it speak our language. Yet this makes it all the more surprising that Harman's own system frames time in terms of a living present rather than letting the present wither away to a vanishing point as Augustine does.

How then shall we position Augustine alongside the twenty-first-century debate between Harman and DeLanda about time's reality? First of all, according to Augustine, the temporal must be thought in relation to the eternal, construed not as the everlasting but rather as that which is beyond time. This puts him out of step with modern thinkers like DeLanda, who rule out the notion of the timeless altogether. All the same, Augustine's strict sense of divine eternity liberates him from the desire to reshape temporality in the image of the timeless (as Harman risks doing). It makes his account of time properly temporal. The present is not a microscopic replica of eternity, but rather an illusion, powerless in the face of the temporal continuum.

Secondly, Augustine is more anthropocentric than any object-oriented ontologist or neo-materialist should be. This is not to say that he is committed to idealism in any modern sense. Still, his primary concern remains the effect that time has upon the human mind. His solution, however, incorporates the insight that the mind, like the rest of nature, is subject to the force of *distentio*. He is a realist about time, even if he is most concerned about the belated effects that time's reality has upon humankind. Augustine, attentive to the embodied character of these effects, links belatedness not just to cognition, but also to the sense of the flesh. This falls short of making Augustine a DeLanda-style materialist, since Augustine would never reduce cognition to the realm of matter alone. As a result, he is neither an idealist about time nor a thoroughgoing materialist about temporal experience. Instead, he is a realist about both time and eternity, even as he remains skeptical of our ability to fully comprehend either time or eternity in this life.

Taking *distentio* as an objective feature of the cosmos, Augustine avoids reducing time to anyone's subjective temporal experience. Removing the real present from the cosmological timeline, he is also able to avoid the spurious notion of a living present. As a result, he can be said to hold an account of time that is both anti-presentist and objective. It makes sense to speak of time itself, even if we struggle to fully grasp it as an object. What then are we speaking of, if not time's force and nature? And what is time's force and nature, if not the natural force of *distentio* it transitively enacts upon us? Time is objective. And we, oddly enough, are its objects.

2

A Brief Theology of Time

From Creation to the Eschaton

Introduction

The February 19, 1933 edition of the *New York Times Magazine* featured an interview with a Belgian priest named Georges Lemaître. The headline ran: "Lemaître Follows Two Paths: the Famous Physicist, Who is Also a Priest, Tells Why He Finds No Conflict Between Science and Religion." Duncan Aikman, the *Times* reporter, tracked Lemaître down while the latter was working in Pasadena. He came to California to work not as a cleric, but as a mathematical physicist and theoretical cosmologist. Lemaître would later be remembered for his theory of the primeval atom, which argued that the best explanation for the origin of the universe was that everything began from some point of infinite density (the aforementioned atom), out of which the rest of the matter and energy in the universe exploded at the beginning of what we know as space-time. By putting this theory forward, Lemaître anticipated the findings of Roger Penrose and Stephen Hawking, whose work concerning black holes made the likelihood of an infinite singularity in nature more plausible, like a primeval atom preceding a big bang (Farrell 2005: 206). Lemaître, never warming to the big bang as a phrase, preferred to speak of the origin in terms of "fireworks" (Ostriker and Mitton 2013).

The years between Lemaître and Hawking, however, saw a number of physicists proclaiming their incredulity over the primeval atom. They saw it as creation *ex nihilo*, suspiciously cast in new guise by a Catholic priest (Farrell 2005: 204–5). In both cases, the universe would begin from a point before which the mind could not see. The first day of creation would thus be "a day without a yesterday" or "the now without a yesterday" (Lemaître 1950: 133). In 1933, the journalist Aikman was acutely aware of the potential for either collusion or conflict between science and religion. The "Bible says that creation was accomplished in six days," he said to Lemaître. "Isn't that a direct, literal statement?" To this, the priest responded (Lambert 2000: 164–5):

> What of it? There is no reason to abandon the Bible because we now believe that it took perhaps ten thousand million years to create what we think is the universe. Genesis is simply trying to teach us that one day in seven should be devoted to rest, worship, and reverence—all necessary to salvation.

Lemaître's blunt response suggests that, for him, there is no conflict between religion and science on creation. Genesis should be read as practical wisdom for humankind, not as an ancient blueprint for the cosmos. "There were two ways of arriving at the truth," remarked Lemaître (Lambert 2000: 165), "I decided to follow them both."

The context of Augustine's account of time in the *Confessions* makes it clear that he, too, was struggling with the question of how best to rectify Genesis with a convincing description of the cosmos. Unlike Lemaître, though, he did not want to reduce Scripture to an advice pamphlet. He agreed that the days of creation in Genesis are figurative, but what they represent is nevertheless a cosmic backstory. This figurative backstory, far from being pure myth, lends itself to rational interpretation, even if certain mysteries stay concealed. For Augustine, there is an objective, natural account of the cosmos standing in contrast to mythopoetic alternatives. His target here is the group to which he and his dead friend once belonged: the Manichaeans, a Jesus-revering movement with roots in the third-century teachings of the prophet Mani. Manichaean cosmology was a tempting alternative to the terse tale told in Genesis 1. In his younger days, Augustine saw in Mani's myths an invitation to a rational appreciation of the structure of the cosmos. By the time he was finishing his *Confessions*, however, Augustine had been disillusioned by his underwhelming encounters with traveling Manichaean intellectuals like Faustus and Fortunatus. His debates with such figures seldom led to any further insights into nature. As a result, he felt emboldened to offer his own account of the beginnings of the universe. Augustine, like Lemaître, began his cosmogonic account with a day that had no yesterday.

Manichaean Cosmology

Before returning to the cosmological scene of the *Confessions*, it would be helpful to sketch out some Manichaean views. As Jason BeDuhn (2000: 72) has pointed out, to speak of a unified Manichaean cosmology would presume too much. What we have in hand are fragmented manuscripts in languages ranging from Syriac and Persian to Chinese. Nevertheless, general tendencies do shine through, such as the moralization of the cosmos, the proliferation of intermediate beings with creative roles to play, and the centrality of Jesus in the awakening of souls to their eschatological salvation.

Elements of Manichaean cosmology are scattered throughout the surviving manuscripts, but Nicholas Baker-Brian (2011: 108–9) has suggested that the fullest account is found in Theodore bar Koni's eighth-century anti-Manichaean polemic. The fact that we reconstruct the details of Manichaean myth by way of its opponents, whether Theodore or Augustine, is a sad reminder of how much we still have to learn about Manichaeism. If we are to trust Theodore and similar sources, however, we can get a sense of how Manichaean theology and cosmology developed in tandem. In the beginning, to steal a phrase, were light and darkness. There is no neutral monist substrate before these two principles. From a Manichaean perspective, the beginning is not a point, but already a duration. Similarly, the Manichaean deity is not eternal in Augustine's strict sense, but "supra-temporal" or omni-temporal (Baker-Brian 2011: 118). Gazing back into the absolute past, all we would see is the everlasting contrast between the light of goodness and the darkness of evil. The balance of these two principles could only be upset by some catastrophe, which unfortunately did occur. The darkness, envious of the light, invaded the kingdom of goodness, ruled over by the original Father. The pre-history of the universe commences with this catastrophe. From the very beginning, Manichaean cosmogony is a moralizing drama playing out between the divine personifications of goodness and evil.

In the wake of this primordial catastrophe arise a proliferation of archons and other beings involved in the creation of the universe as we know it. These lesser divinities are derived from the initial response of the Father, which cannot consist in violent reprisal against the invasion of his territory, since that would sully the light with a dark stratagem. According to one popular version, the Father's first step is to conceptually spawn the Mother, in a manner reminiscent of non-sexual reproduction in Valentinian and Sethian theogonies. The Mother then spawns the First Man, who is not yet a man in any this-worldly sense, but instead the prototype of what humankind could be in its most spiritually de-materialized instantiation. The First Man, a pacifist like his Father, allows himself and his own Sons to be consumed by the forces of darkness. Augustine's Manichaean rival Fortunatus explicitly linked the First Man's self-sacrifice to Christ's self-emptying kenosis in Phil. 2:5-8 (Baker-Brian 2011: 112). While this seems like an example of divine vulnerability, its greater purpose is to kick-start salvation history, since the sparks of light consumed by dark archons will ultimately be the undoing of the darkness itself.

Lying dormant within the dark for a time, these sparks are destined to be saved by a sophisticated rescue effort on the part of the divine. At this point, the proliferation of divine entities reaches fever pitch. The most important of these is the Living Spirit. By creating the rest of the cosmos as we come to encounter it, with its eight earths and no less than ten heavens, these demiurgic figures play a key role in helping the light escape from its prison. Despite what some critics said, creation was thus a good thing in the Manichaean view. This is one of the characteristics distinguishing Mani's followers from a host of other dualistic groups in antiquity.

Creation remains, however, a drawn-out process, its beauty tempered by periodic eruptions of violence. The feminized Living Spirit, for example, sacrificially permits itself to be inseminated by darkness, leading to the creation of the partially material sun and moon. The trick is that sun and moon also play saving roles, since both reflect the light of souls trapped on earth back up to their homeland. "The universe serves as an astral machine geared towards the purification of the Living Soul as light" (Baker-Brian 2011: 113). The solar system becomes a celestial water-wheel, scooping droplets of light up from earth, elevating them to the moon and sun, then setting them free in a realm no darkness can reach. An-Nadim, a tenth-century Muslim chronicler of Manichaeism, reported in his *Fihrist* that Mani's followers saw this process as culminating in a purgative and emancipatory fire (Be Duhn 2000: 76). Another violent episode of Manichaean salvation-history has feminized archons releasing aborted offspring in order to be inseminated anew. The resulting abortions are then eaten by two more archons, Ashqalun and Namrael, who then copulate in order to produce Adam and Eve. The simplicity of the narrative in Genesis 1–2 is rapidly receding out of view.

All too often, the sophistication of this cosmology is misrepresented as proof that Manichaeism is not Christian. Yet even the briefest perusal of Manichaean texts reveals that Jesus remains central, though he takes many forms over the course of salvation-history. It is Jesus the Suffering, for example, who allows his living soul to be disseminated in the darkness. It is Jesus the Splendour, meanwhile, who reveals to Adam that he is a soul trapped within crude matter. And it is also Jesus the Splendour who will return in the end to judge humankind. Manichaean cosmology thus takes us all the way from a cosmogonic origin, through the tragedy of human existence, down to a final threshing of the wheat from the chaff. Historically, the Manichaean system played out in terms of what BeDuhn calls the "three times": the initial time of purified separation; the damnable epoch of illegitimate intermixing; and the ultimate era of redemptive re-separation. BeDuhn (2013: 375) further suggests that the "three times" decried by Augustine in *Confessions* 11, which appear on the surface to be the colloquial past, present, and future, also denote these three periods of Manichaean history.

One of the most detailed Manichaean cosmologies is found in the *Šabuhragan*, a text presented by Mani to the Sassanian court of Shapur. There Mani tells us that Jesus the Splendour will judge most harshly those who abused the vegetarian Manichaean ascetics known as the elect, who will go to paradise, perhaps along with their audience of helpers, the hearers (who might pass through a few cycles of reincarnation first). The archons, meanwhile, will burn for almost 1,500 years, exhausting every bit of light left in them before they are sent back to everlasting darkness. Most of us live on the cusp of liberation and hellfire, in the "interim" between Jesus' revelation to Adam and his splendiferous return (BeDuhn 2000: 73; Baker-Brian 2011: 116). Even as we work toward supposed progress, we remain caught in this mixed-up context, where light can appear as dark and dark as light. Accordingly, the Manichaean "interim" might anticipate what Augustine will later call the *saeculum*.

For now, let us end this recapitulation of Mani's cosmology by agreeing with BeDuhn and Baker-Brian that the Manichaean worldview was not fully deterministic. Near the end of Augustine's life, his opponent Julian of Eclanum would accuse him of being a closeted Manichaean, importing dualistic predestination into Christian virtue ethics. The Manichaeans, however, seldom preached determinism. Admittedly, non-human forms of agency, including the work of good entities and dark archons, as well as astrological influence, did play a role. All the same, responsibility lay with the human soul, which had to choose between good and evil, aiding in its own liberation or yielding to its own imprisonment. Once again, cosmology brings us back to the moral arc of the universe.

Nevertheless, the cosmic context of moral agency remains. Manichaeans in late antiquity need only have gazed up into the night sky to confirm their beliefs. There the moon awaited to confirm the mythopoetic framework laid out by their prophet. Light returning to light sounds like a metaphor but, in the end, it is no metaphor at all. That was what Augustine came to learn through debates with Manichaeans like Fortunatus and Faustus, as he reports in *Confessions* 5. He had hoped that beneath the surface of the myths resided some rational account of nature or at least the professional astrology in which he himself dabbled. That was not the case. Mani's cosmogonic myths were not meant to be unraveled by clever minds. Nor were they reducible to astrology as conventionally calculated (BeDuhn 2009: 97). They were literal narratives articulating the moral quandary faced by humankind in this battleground of a cosmos (Baker-Brian 2011: 100–4).

Manichaean resistance to figuratively rendering their own myths rational need not derive from anti-intellectualism. BeDuhn (2009: 125) argues that Faustus' resistance to rationalizing interpretations was fueled by Ciceronian skepticism. What Mani and the academy shared was a sense that our sensory impressions are illusory. That could also be why Manichaeanism integrated so easily with Buddhist teachings. Yet while the skeptic and the Manichaean agreed on the untrustworthiness of phenomenal data, they presented distinct solutions. For Cicero, a pragmatic approach won out: practical wisdom could be expressed with confidence in a way that theoretical speculations (including astronomical reflections on the cosmos) never could. For Faustus, meanwhile, the collapse of rational reflection into bottomless skepticism only proved that theoretically compelling solutions were hard to come by. In the absence of any rationally provable cosmology, the myths of Mani were as compelling as any other.

A Day Without a Yesterday

The context of Augustine's account of time reveals it to be a contribution to ancient cosmology, which we have just met in Manichaean garb. The first nine books of the *Confessions* depict scenes from Augustine's personal history to make a broader point about humankind's dependency on a created cosmos. Augustine does this by confessing his recollections to the God he now recognizes as his Creator. His use of confession and praise, both of which address God in the second person, is rife with Scriptural references, so intricately woven into the text that it is difficult to distinguish Augustine's voice from what he is citing. *Confessions* 11 fits into this flow of the overall work. It, too, is a confession of praise to the Creator. It, too, approaches its themes by way of a biblical guide. In fact, it goes further, serving as an exegesis of the opening of Genesis, which makes sense, since Augustine is working toward the climax of his reflection on what it feels like to be created. The goal of interrogating time was to understand these words: "In the beginning, God created heaven and earth."

It is not enough, however, to recast Augustine's account of temporality as exegesis. Questions about the beginning of the universe led Augustine to reflect on themes that are not apparent to most readers of Genesis 1. Taking a few steps back from the chapters dealing with the problem of the present should allow us to take a closer look at how Augustine arrived at these questions. The first nine chapters of *Confessions* 11 deepen our understanding of what it could mean for the beginning (*principium*) of the universe to be identical to God's Word or Wisdom. The tenth through thirteenth chapters heighten the stakes, arguing that misunderstanding the nature of this cosmic beginning leads to a misinterpretation of creation, which proves fatal if it causes us to confuse the temporality of the world with the timelessness of God. From the fourteenth chapter on, Augustine assumes this timeless eternity of the Creator as a framework for posing the problem of time, which brings us back to the inescapability of *distentio* and belatedness. But let us now begin again from the first chapter of *Confessions* 11.

After ten books spent confessing, Augustine begins the eleventh by acknowledging the absurdity of it all. He is confessing his sins and his prayers to a God who already knows these things in timeless eternity. God does not learn anything from Augustine's speaking in time. So why do it? Augustine (CF 11.1.1) asserts that he has confessed because God "wanted" him to.[1] But even if doing God's will means confessing, does that make it wise to use up so many "drops of time" (*stillae temporum*) writing those confessions down (CF 11.2.2)? If God does not learn through human speech, the case should be the same for human letters. Yet Augustine (CF 11.2.3) says he is composing these books in service of "brotherly love" (*fraternae caritati*). His confessions are to God but for his readers. Augustine next asks for the grace which he may have already received, since only by this gift can he illuminate the opacity of Scripture to help his brothers and sisters understand God's message. Appealing to God, he writes (CF 11.2.3): "Let me confess to you whatever I will have found in your books."[2] This appeal to the divine must occur through the Mediator, Christ, who was present at the universe's first stirrings. Only the Word made flesh holds the keys to unlocking the mysteries of the Word as Scripture.

"Let me hear and understand," Augustine prays (CF 11.3.5), "how 'in the beginning you made heaven and earth.'"[3] Though he asks this in humility, seeking access to the secrets of Genesis is not the humblest of requests. With Scripture as his authority, Augustine already believes that the account of creation in Genesis is true. What he does not understand, though, is how it could possibly be true. He believes but does not understand. In search of understanding, he has to interpret Genesis according to some standard of truth, which is what allows him to determine whether any claims (in speech, in writing, even in Scripture) are true or false. Though Augustine finds this standard of truth within himself, he also holds truth to be God. As Christ put it: "I am the way, the truth, and the life" (Jn. 14:6). Augustine's plea for God's grace is a plea for aid from the truth itself.

Having risen to an awareness of this need for a standard of truth, Augustine comes back down to heaven and earth. Speaking alongside Scripture is the book of nature, in which heaven and earth get a chance to speak for themselves, announcing to Augustine that they are changeable creatures. How they currently are is not how they used to be. From this, he infers that they did not make themselves. Their instability must be derived from something stabler (CF 11.4.6):

> See that the heaven and the earth are. They cry out that they were made, for they are changed and varied. Whatever is not made and yet is, however, has nothing in it which was not so before (that is what it means to be changed or varied). Heaven and earth cry out, too, that they did not make themselves: "And so we are because we were made. This means that we were not before we were, so that we could not have been made by ourselves."[4]

In other words, heaven and earth were created by the God of Genesis, who is immutable in a way that the Manichaean divinities are not. But since God gave all things in heaven and earth their being, God's own being could never be the same as theirs. Compared to God, all such things are not. Temporal mutability bears little resemblance to its divine source. Augustine next rules out the possibility that God, like a human craftsman, took raw material and made it into something else. There was no pre-existent material with which to build (CF 12.3–8). Augustine's God was not a demiurgic builder, but the creator *ex nihilo*. The divine medium was not mud but speech. "You spoke and they were made," confesses Augustine (CF 11.5.7). "You made them in your word."[5] Divine speech enables God to create without needing anything external with which to create.

This raises the question of what it means for God to speak. In the gospel, Augustine (CF 11.6.8) finds an example in the voice that says of Christ: "This is my beloved son" (Mt. 3:17; 17:5). But this was heard by human ears. It was uttered temporally, syllable by syllable over a span of time. It cannot be the speaking that brought time into being in the first place. Therefore, Augustine holds that this evangelical utterance was spoken by means of a temporal intermediary. It is not a clue leading us in the direction of the original Word, by which God created heaven and earth. Primordial divine speech, insofar as it created time, would have to be atemporal, unlike speech as we know it. Instead of unfolding in time, God's Word is always saying all that it says (CF 11.7.9). Heaven and earth and everything in them are always being said in that Word, even though those things arise and pass away in time. The Word is eternal, but what it creates is not. But how can the arising and passing away of things relate to a timeless Word? Augustine tentatively suggests a relation modeled on the keeping of accounts (CF 11.8.10):

> I see it in one way or another, but I do not know how to express it, except to say that everything which begins to be and ceases begins to be and ceases at the time when it is thought that it ought to begin or cease. This thinking takes place in the eternal calculation, where nothing begins or ceases. This itself is your Word, which is the beginning, since it also speaks to us.[6]

The timeless Word is the ledger keeping track of the temporal debt of all things. This debt is calculated on the basis of the time things receive (i.e., how long they ought to exist or the time they are owed) and the time that is taken away from them. Augustine's wordplay is predicated on the fact that the Greek *logos* can be rendered into Latin as both a word (*verbum*) and an account (*ratio*): that is, a calculated reckoning-up of all things, according to their allotted measure of existence. This is the same Word that, in *Confessions* 4, announced to every thing that it is permitted to exist "from here up to here" and no further.

Even after clarifying the relationship between Word and world, Augustine is still confused by God's creative speech. That God created heaven and earth through his Word strikes him as true, even though he cannot understand how it could be true. It strikes him as true because wisdom (*sapientia*) has spoken up within him, like an interior voice resonating from elsewhere. Augustine identifies this wisdom with the principle (*principium*) of all things, the stable truth to which we return after wandering down the path of thinking, and with the beginning (*principium*) through which all things were made. Wisdom, truth, principle, and beginning: all of these names are revealed to be secret identities of the divine Word. "How magnificent your works are, Lord," cries Augustine (CF 11.9.11), quoting Ps. 104:24. "You made all things in wisdom!" His cause for exclamation is the recognition that he must come to learn about the Word, Wisdom, and Principle (through which all things were created) by appealing to the Word, Wisdom, and Principle (through which humankind comes to learn the truth about all things).

Having clarified the role of the Word in creation, Augustine is ready to counter a conventional criticism of Gen. 1:1. There are some, he says, who are so "full of their own oldness" that they stubbornly question Scripture's first sentence. Augustine (CF 11.10.12) notes that, in response to the claim that God made heaven and earth "in the beginning," these critics try to get back before this absolute starting-point in order to ask: "What was God doing before he made the heaven and the earth?"[7] The short version of Augustine's answer is that, since time was created alongside the world, there was no "before creation." Far from merely directing the seasons, God made time itself (CF 11.13.15). The first day of the hexaemeron really was a day without a yesterday. Yet a subtler line of questioning is also in play. If creation is an eternal decision in the will of God, why is the created world not everlasting? If God is always creating, then how come heaven and earth will not always be? Skeptical questions like these could have been asked by Augustine's former Manichaean allies. In their view, simply reciting Gen. 1:1 would be insufficient to silence the complexities of Mani's cosmogony.

Contrary to some accounts, Augustine does not respond to these questions with scorn. He refuses to respond with the joke often misattributed to him (CF 11.12.14): "Before God created heaven and earth, he was making hell for those who would ask such questions." Instead, he says it is fair game to discuss the creation of the universe. The problem with the "old men" above is that they speak vaguely, failing to understand the distinction between this world's time and God's timelessness. Augustine expresses sympathy for these misguided people, who speculate about time and eternity even as they are caught up within temporal instability (CF 11.11.13):

They don't understand how those things are made which are made through you and in you. They try to know eternal things, but their heart is still flying around in the past and future movements of things. Their heart is still empty. Who will hold it and fix it in place, so that it can stand a little bit and grasp, just a little bit, the splendour of eternity, which is always standing? So that it can compare eternity with the times, which never stand, and see that they are incomparable? So that it can see that a long time does not become long except out of many movements which pass away and are not able to be stretched out all at once? And that in the eternal, moreover, nothing passes away, but rather the whole is present? That no time is truly present as a whole? That everything that has passed away is thrown forth out of what will be, and that everything that will be follows out of what has passed away? And that everything that has passed away or will be is created by and runs out of that which is always present? Who will hold the human heart so that it stands and sees how standing eternity, which neither has passed by nor will be, says over and over again both the times to come and those which have passed away?[8]

The questions of the old ones, Augustine is saying, are predicated on a false association between eternity and everlastingness. They presume that the eternity of God's creative Word should correspond to some everlastingness in what that Word creates. But this is to misinterpret eternity. God's Word is not eternal because it goes on forever. It is strictly timeless, whereas the created world is pervaded by time (CF 11.13.16; Rogers 1994). Temporality conditions every aspect of the created. Augustine emphasizes the impermanence of all things, including human hearts and minds, caught up in the flux of a time that is never fully present. Even an everlasting creation would still be made up of a sequence of movements, all of which would pass away just as they arise, lacking any ability to stand still. Motion is fluid, without instantaneous points or stable units. The same goes for the time in which motion takes place. This temporality could never apply to God's timelessness, which lies beyond even the everlasting flight of unstable mobility.

The Cosmic Spring

The account of creation that Augustine offers in the *Confessions* thus differs considerably from Manichaean cosmogony. Gone are the two divine principles, replaced by the unitary principle of the Trinity in its self-relation. God speaks God the Word as God the Spirit moves over the waters. The Mother, the First Man, and the Living Spirit fall silent. In addition to this change in the cast of characters, the more fundamental shift is Augustine's abandonment of the idea of a deity that lasts forever (like Mani's Father of Light) in favor of an eternity altogether outside time. If the Manichaeans were asking what God was doing before creating, they would have had their own response ready to hand (BeDuhn 2013: 374). Before the creation of this world, the good God was abiding in a kingdom of light, unsullied by the forces of darkness lying in wait. Mani's myth could use human language, with its tenses and aspects, to describe what God was doing before the creation of this universe. The first epoch of the Manichaean "three times" cosmology could extend backward indefinitely, since light and darkness had always been separate, and would have remained so if not for a primal catastrophe. By the time of the composition of the *Confessions*, Augustine was fed up with the complications of this cosmogony and with the idea that any God worth the name could endure in time, waiting on future events to happen, rather than standing outside time in singular serenity.

Even earlier, in his debates with the Manichaean orator Faustus, Augustine had expressed his incredulity at Manichaean cosmology. "That myth of yours is long and foolish, a child's plaything," he raved (Baker-Brian 2011: 102), "containing a truncated beginning, a rotten middle, and a ruinous end." However, as we know, what Augustine found when he challenged Faustus was a man just as skeptical as himself. Faustus not only declined to defend Mani's narrative on rational grounds, but even suggested that there was no point in engaging in speculative cosmology whatsoever. The idea that humankind might rise to the level of understanding the unfathomable mysteries of the universe struck an academic fellow-traveler like Faustus as absurd. The Manichaean story was not meant to be the final word on natural science. Mani was a pragmatic prophet. The everlasting war of light against dark was true in the sense that it helps us make sense of the human predicament, torn apart as we are between an invitation to goodness and the forces dragging us down to hell. Perhaps, then, the sun and the moon were not the result of divine intercourse. But if we could still look up into the sky and be reminded of the possibility of liberation from evil's pull, then Mani's mythopoetic cosmogony remained powerful.

Augustine, in both the *Contra Faustum* and the *Confessions*, adopts the opposite approach. For him, it matters that Mani's myth is untrue. Recall what he said near the beginning of *Confessions* 11 about the synonymy of truth, wisdom, and principle with Christ. The truth that is Christ is not to be taken lightly. Of course, Augustine also went through a skeptical period. But this only reinforced his desire to find something that was really true. While the main aim of his desire for truth was theological, the same drive colored his approach to cosmology and temporality. The origin of the universe mattered. The nature of time was worthy of consideration. This sincere interest in cosmology drove Augustine's interest in astrology, which, as BeDuhn (2009: 123) reminds us, was hardly distinguishable from astronomy in antiquity. The Manichaean system found only limited room for astrology as popularly practiced, which might surprise us, given Mani's association with the stars. Yet the choice made by each person to either cultivate the light or embrace the darkness far outweighed the moderate influence stars have on human action. Augustine was not satisfied with this dismissal of the relationship between the cosmos and those who live within the cosmos. He seldom treated life as an open-ended adventure in free choice, with the possible exception of some texts written between 388 and 396 CE (BeDuhn 2009: 264–5). Nevertheless, Augustine was happy to abandon astrology in his post-conversion life. In the long run, this abandonment amounted to a rejection not of the external conditions placed on human agency, but of the stars as privileged means for the discernment of those conditions.

Augustine's rejection of astrology is certainly not a rejection of speculative cosmology. To investigate the origins of the universe is no sin. Nor is it, as Faustus thought, pointless. For Augustine, there is no shame in thinking back to the beginning, even as it recedes to an unimaginable point beyond which lies timeless eternity. Lemaître (1950: 141–2) referred to this as that drive through which, "by means of thought, one wishes to attempt to retrace the course of time." In the *Confessions*, Augustine traces cosmic history backward in the barest of outlines. In *Confessions* 12, for example, he mentions the immaterial "heaven of heavens" preceding the universe not in time but according to the hierarchy of reason; the opposite of this *caelum caeli* is "unformed matter," which God must make in order to construct the rest of the universe, but which also does not fit into the flux of forms characteristic of the passage of time (CF 12.2.2–12.8.8). Angels, too, occupy an awkward patch of middle ground between time and timelessness, since they are neither eternal like the Trinity nor susceptible to *distentio*, held close as they are to God in the quasi-eternity or sempiternity gracing the heaven of heavens (CF 12.11.12).

Augustine goes into greater detail in *The Literal Meaning of Genesis*, the latest of his anti-Manichaean attempts to make sense of the first passages of Scripture. There he clarifies that the six days of creation are in fact one day (DG 1.9.15–17; 5.3.5). This one, time-bending day of creation is in turn identified with the knowledge the angels have of what the Dominican translator Edmund Hill (Augustine 2002: 174–5, 278–9) called the "formulae" (*rationes*) of all things contained in God's Word. This means that, "before" the temporal aspects of creation (say, the spiralling-outward of the galaxies), there was "already" an immaterial creation which, again, preceded the cosmos not in time but in the rational order of causation. Augustine (2002: 294; DG 5.17.35) stresses that this original creation was simultaneous, whereas the ongoing history of cosmic providence unfolds over time. The fact that a spiritual creation "precedes" the material creation of the universe does not mean there was an actual "yesterday" before the "first day" or the beginning of time and space. To borrow again from the elegant translation of Hill (Augustine 2002: 282; DG 5.5.12): "it is time that begins from the creation, rather than the creation from time." By allegorizing the word "day" into angelic knowledge of the cosmic paradigm, Augustine reaffirms his anti-Manichaean sense that the universe began with a bang.

In the fifth book of *The Literal Meaning of Genesis*, Augustine clarifies that his metaphor for time's beginning is not explosive, as it would be for Lemaître, but hydrological, in keeping with the river of time. If we trace this river back to its origin, however, we find the "spring" (*fons*) mentioned in Gen. 2:6. This "spring," says Augustine (using a figure of speech also found in the *City of God*), acts as a "joint" (*articulus*) in Scripture, around which two modes of creation hinge (DG 5.11.27; Augustine 2002: 289). On the anterior side of the joint, we find *creatio simul*: the simultaneous, spiritual creation that takes place timelessly in the Word and in view of the angels; on the posterior side of the joint lies the temporal universe, which continues to be guided by a creative intelligence, although the gears of providence remain obscure to us (as will be the case again in the

City of God). Returning once more to Hill (Augustine 2002: 290; DG 5.11.27), we find: "From this mention of this spring onwards, whatever the narrative tells of was henceforth done through periods of time, not 'all things simultaneously.'" Instead of a big bang, Augustine posits a big spring, bursting forth out of the divine abyss of creation just as explosively as Lemaître's fireworks. Augustine thereby articulates his version of a "day without a yesterday" in terms of this singular spring.

It is the seriousness with which Augustine treats speculative cosmology in both *The Literal Meaning of Genesis* and *Confessions* 11 that keeps him in conversation with even modern physics insofar as it is grounded in Lemaître's theory. Whereas Augustine, like Aristotle, thought of time as a line, by Lemaître's age the cone of space-time had become the fashionable image. "We can compare space-time to an open, conic cup," remarked Lemaître (1950: 133). "The bottom of the cup is the origin of atomic disintegration; it is the first instant at the bottom of space-time, the now which has no yesterday because, yesterday, there was no space." While the framework has obviously changed, thanks to the importation of zero into European mathematics and the advent of infinitesimal calculus, there remains a resonance between Augustine and Lemaître. It is the echo of a day without a yesterday.

In the parlance of the Belgian priest, the *principium* was not a divine *logos* but a cosmic *atomos*: something that could not be or had not yet been cut apart. As Lemaître explained (Lambert 2000: 120):

> Here the word "atom" should be understood in the primitive Greek sense of the word. It is intended to mean absolute simplicity, excluding any multiplicity. The atom is so simple that nothing can be said about it and no question raised. It provides a beginning which is entirely inaccessible. It is only when it has split up into a large number of fragments by filling up a space of small, but not strictly zero radius, that physical notions begin to acquire some meaning.

The primeval atom is ineffable, if not quite divine. It is not an atom in the commonly accepted sense of the term in physics today. Its roots are ancient, both cosmologically and philologically speaking. Its necessity is mathematical in nature (Lambert 2000: 161–4). As a result, the primeval atom served as a building block even in the new world of relativity and quantum physics carved out by Einstein and Bohr. Have we thereby returned to Augustine's universe, in which everything finds its temporal account already reckoned up in the timeless calculation of the divine *logos* or *ratio*?

Despite these Augustinian resonances, Lemaître is operating in a different universe. In addition to calculus and relativity, Lemaître also happens to be living in the wake of the Reformation, the Council of Trent, and Neo-Scholasticism. This may have played some role in his refusal to reduce the universe to a preordained process of atomic decay. "[T]he whole story of the world need not have been written down in the first quantum like a song on the disc of a phonograph," said Lemaître. "The whole matter of the world must have been present at the beginning, but the story it has to tell may be written step by step" (Lambert 2000: 121). We should be reminded of Augustine's musings on song. In *Confessions* 10, song is a means of temptation. Hymns lure Augustine's focus away from the immutable God with their lyrical mutability. In the middle of *Confessions* 11, singing a song exemplifies the ongoing interplay of *memoria*, *contuitus*, and *exspectatio* that must be occurring if the human soul is going to be held together amidst the flux of time. Most relevant is a question asked near the end of *Confessions* 11. If the human experience of getting stretched out were extended unendingly in both directions, would that constitute a consciousness equivalent to God? The Augustinian response must be in the negative. According to Lemaître, the song was not composed *in principio*; for Augustine, however, the song of the universe was indeed composed, even if singing it from beginning to end would not make the singer a god.

For Lemaître, this divergence from Augustine was more of a feature than a bug. He had no desire to upset the scientific establishment or raise concerns about his ulterior motives as a Vatican agent. No doubt the words of Einstein had been ringing in his ears since the day Lemaître first told him of the primeval atom, to which the theorist of relativity responded: "No, not that, that suggests too much the creation" (Farrell 2005: 100). Lemaître's embarrassment only increased with the 1952 publication of Pius XII's *Ora*, in which the Pontiff remarked: "it would seem that present-day science, with one sweep back across the centuries, has succeeded in bearing witness to the august instant of the *Fiat Lux*, when, along with matter, there burst forth from nothing a sea of light and radiation, and the elements split and churned and formed into millions of galaxies" (Farrell 2005: 196). Setting aside for the moment the fact that Augustine associated *fiat lux* with the angels rather than with the creation of the temporal universe, we can still appreciate the Augustinian resonances in Pius' attempt to link physics with theology. Lemaître was unmoved. For him, the science closest to theology was not physics, but psychology, the discipline aimed at healing the soul.

Conclusion

Unlike Lemaître, Augustine held out hope that the logic of the cosmos and the fate of the soul could come back into communion. As he concluded *Confessions* 11 by lamenting time as *distentio*, Augustine returned to his Manichaean questions once more. His longing for eschatological stability reinvigorated his opposition to navel-gazing over a time before creation. Against this he asserted (CF 11.30.40) that "there can be no time without creation."[9] The two are joined at the hip by a creator standing outside temporality. As purely timeless, God's knowledge and activity are utterly unlike ours. There is no analogy. When we sing a song, we do so thanks to the imperfect interplay of memory, awareness, and expectation. The same is not true of the deity. "Far be it from me," says Augustine (CF 11.31.41) to God, "to imply that You, composer of the universe, composer of living souls and bodies, know all things that will be and have been like I know a song! You are far stranger and far more secret."[10] Eternity, for Augustine, is atemporal, not everlasting. If we have trouble grasping what that could mean, since our ways of talking and thinking and feeling are inextricably time-bound, that fact too is instructive.

In *Confessions* 12, Augustine makes a remark that helps us break his terminology down into a triad. The first is that of memory (*memoria*), awareness (*contuitus*), and expectation (*exspectatio*). The second triad, which does not map onto the first, is: stretching-apart (*distentio*), stretching-out (*extentio*), and stretching-toward (*intentio*). For Augustine, *intentio* denotes the basic directedness of the soul in its temporal life. Is *intentio* therefore capable of transforming *distentio* (destructive stretching-apart) into *extentio* (redemptive stretching-outward)? Can we "focus" our way into a better, stabler mode of temporal experience? A conclusion like that strains the limits of Augustine's cosmological imagination. Augustine (CF 12.15.18) instead writes: "The expectation of things to come becomes, when those things come, awareness [*contuitus*]. Likewise, awareness becomes memory when those things have passed away. Every *intentio*, which is varied in this way, is mutable."[11]

It turns out that *intentio*, far from liberating us from time, is also subject to variation and mutability. Neither *intentio* nor the experiential triad (of memory, awareness, and expectation) can reconstitute a stable present in which we could take hold of time and make it our own. A soul's intentionality remains caught in time's currents. Instead of an escape from time, we have a distended intentionality.

Distentio does a lot of psychological and cosmological work for Augustine. That is why its meaning matters. If we had taken *distentio animi* as a subjective genitive, for example, it might have struck us as the soul's achievement. Widening outward, the soul would construct for itself an island of presence in the midst of time's river. If we consider Augustine's account of time in its cosmological context, however, such an interpretation becomes untenable. *Distentio* is the objective force of cosmic time stretching the soul apart. This has consequences. First of all, the soul can no longer be described as existing in the present alone. Nor can it be said to exist in discrete phases matching the linguistic tenses. Memory does not neatly correspond to the past. Awareness does not fit into a point-like now. Expectation does not reveal the depths of the future. Rather, all three coexist as modes of the soul's temporal experience, which is itself a response to the continuum of objective, cosmological time. Unfortunately for us, the soul's distended situation goes hand in hand with a feeling of distracted instability. *Distentio* cannot fix this, but reflecting on *distentio* can liberate us from the illusion that we are trapped in a fleeting moment. Liberation comes at the cost of acknowledging how caught up we are in the torrent of time, grasping after what has just passed away while being drawn inexorably into the future.

3

Enlightenment Never

Eschatology Without Progress

Introduction

In his 2018 book *Enlightenment Now: The Case for Reason, Science, Humanism, and Progress*, psychologist Steven Pinker argues that now is the best time to be alive. To support his case, Pinker (2018: 37) quotes from Barack Obama, who said that if "you had to choose blindly what moment you'd want to be born, you'd choose now." Pinker's evidence is drawn from fields like medical science, which have succeeded in increasing measurable criteria like average lifespans. Pinker's case weakens once the reader notices him decoupling certain factors (such as socioeconomic inequality) from the target of human flourishing. According to Pinker (2018: 98), "income inequality is not a fundamental component of well-being." While we could quibble over his manipulations of the data or his definition of the fundamental, the deeper question here is historiographical. How does Pinker ascend from statistical datasets to an overarching judgment about the arc of the moral universe? What is his theory of history?

Pinker presents history in a linear, progressive fashion: each age gets better than the next, especially from the seventeenth century onward. "This heroic story is not just another myth," he adds (2018: 453). "Myths are fictions, but this one is true." But why does Pinker think of history as a progressive timeline? As the example of antiquity proved, it is not immediately clear that we should think of time as linear: perhaps it instead circles back in a pattern of cyclical return. As Karl Löwith suggested in 1949's *Meaning in History*, the fact that people like Pinker think of time as a line is already evidence of the effects of Christianity upon historical consciousness. In Löwith's view, modern linear history is an artefact of Christian eschatology, which flattened the circle of recurrence into a straight line pressing ahead into the future. This view seems borne out by Augustine's *City of God*, which seeks to replace the popular historiographical notions of late antiquity with a linear model. Might Augustine be guilty of taking the first step on a slippery slope leading down towards Pinker's half-baked generalizations?

An examination of Augustine's *City of God* reveals that this is not the case. The Augustinian view of history is linear, but it is not progressive in Pinker's sense. Its linearity is instead to be explained as an extension of the arguments already encountered in the *Confessions*. Augustine's cosmology incorporates subjective time-consciousness, the distensive force of time that conditions the universe, and the linear flow of historical time as experienced by communities living within that universe. But to appreciate the continuity in Augustine's approach to time, we have to turn from the *Confessions* to the *City of God*. This later work also describes temporality in terms of belatedness, not just on the level of an individual lifetime, but now also on the level of history writ large.

Even to sing a simple song, Augustine had said, requires the reality of *distentio* and the subtle interplay of memory, awareness, and expectation. The cosmic history of the universe, however, could not be recited like a song. But what about human history? Is it like a song? The answer initially seems to be yes. According to Augustine (CF 11.28.38):

> What happens in the entire song happens also in its individual parts and syllables. The same thing happens in a longer activity, of which that song is perhaps a part. The same happens in the entirety of a human life, whose parts are all of the actions of one person, and the same happens in the entire age of humankind, whose parts are all human lives.[1]

To liken any human activity to a song is one thing; to liken an entire lifespan to a song is another; and to liken all of history, or at least this age of history, to a song is quite another still. The word

Augustine uses for age is *saeculum*. It is a troublesome word, since its semantic range takes us from "century" to "epoch" and beyond. Decades ago, R. A. Markus' *Saeculum* clarified Augustine's use of this term to refer to the ages of human history, stretching from the first stirrings of Genesis 1 down to the advent of Christ, then into our era, which is defined by its lack of the apparent theological meaning which Scripture revealed to have been present in the epochs of Noah, Abraham, Moses, and the rest. Markus suggested that the age in which we live is a *saeculum* in a special sense: it is more secular than previous *saecula*, insofar as it is no longer clear to humankind what the God-given logic of history is. Providence has dimmed, though not disappeared, for us.

For Augustine, then, time must be linear, insofar as it begins with a bang (or a spring) and ends with an eschaton. The ages of history are also linear: instead of repeating, they drive the work of salvation onward, each new covenant revealing something novel about the relationship between humankind and its divinity. Despite all this linearity, however, Augustine never says that things are getting better in Pinker's sense. Nor, crucially, does he say they are getting worse. The logic of our *saeculum* suggests that things are getting neither better nor worse; they simply tarry alongside us as we live in the wake of divine action and await the arrival of divine respite.

The Empty *Saeculum*

The occasion for writing the first book of the *City of God* was the Sack of Rome carried out by Alaric in 410 CE. According to Augustine, non-Christians blamed this attack on the rise of Christianity within the empire. With the waning of the old rites and the waxing of the new Christian times, the safeguards of civil religion were crumbling. Without the gods to watch over Rome, who could guarantee its future? When these *tempora Christiana* were ruled over by Theodosius, Christians might have replied that their own rise to power coincided with some new golden age. But when the situation grew more volatile, a blindly pro-imperial counterargument in favor of progress became less tenable. As W. H. C. Frend (1989: 15) once phrased it: "Christian times had become what we should call a 'sick joke.'"

Augustine thus had to rethink the meaning of these Christian times. If pagans were calling the present age of history worse than what came before, it would be pointless to assert that things were in fact better. The phrase *tempora Christiana* named a problem, not a solution. What started out as context-specific confusion transformed into an investigation into the meaning of historical events. The Sack of Rome was received by many as a meaningful moment changing the face of history. Most received it as unwelcome; others saw something positive in it. But what the *City of God* tells us is that the meaning of this event remained unclear even to those who lived through it. To quote the extreme formulation of M.B. Pranger (2010: 248): "Alaric's sack of Rome in 410 did not mean anything to" Augustine.

In *City of God* 1, Augustine begins, as usual, with Scripture. He notes that Alaric spared many Romans, Christians, and non-Christians alike. The actions of the Goths, motivated by Arian Christian mercy, injured and benefitted people regardless of their relationship to God. All of this was in keeping with Mt. 5:45, according to Augustine (CD 1.8):

> Someone will say, "So why does divine mercy extend even to the irreligious and ungrateful?" Why do we think this? Perhaps because the one who grants it is the one who daily "makes the sun rise on both the good and the bad, and rains on both the just and the unjust."…It pleased divine providence to hold in reserve those good things which just people will enjoy and unjust people will not. The same goes for those bad things which irreligious people will suffer and good people will not. But providence wanted temporal goods and evils to be common to both, so that we do not desire and seek after what bad people are also seen to have, and so that we do not shamefully avoid what often afflicts even good people.

Augustine emphasizes providence's resistance to rendering judgments on human actions as they occur. This lack of an immediately interpretable result makes moral evaluation difficult. Picking out good from bad is hard if providence is invisible. The notion that people get what they deserve in this life becomes unconvincing. Augustine instead upholds the idea that just deserts are held in reserve (*praeparare in posterum*) until the end of time.

The correct response to this opacity of providence is neither to grow angry with God nor to attain greater clarity. The point is to accept our inability to interpret the meaning of history as it happens. Such interpretation would be an act of judgment, but true judgment happens only in retrospect, long after the deed has been done. Judging the meaning of historical events must await history's end, from which an eschatological eye could gaze back upon the ruins behind it. Like the spring of creation, Augustine (CD 1.12) describes the eschaton as a *punctum*. Both occupy a liminal place in historical time. Since we live along the line stretching out between these two points, the judgments of God strike us as occurring in secret. Augustine cites Rom. 11:33 in support of this: "God's judgments are inscrutable, God's ways are past finding out."

A similar logic animates Augustine's discussion of the two cities, one heavenly and the other earthly. The visible city of God, conceived in terms of the historical church (CD 1.35):

> should clearly remember that its future citizens are hidden among its enemies. It should not think it fruitless that it endures their hostility until they come to confess. Likewise, the city of God holds within itself a number of those who are not going to be in the eternal lot of the saints, though they are connected to the communion of saints as long as they wander through the world.[2]

More optimistically, Augustine continues (CD 1.35):

> So the correction of such people is far from hopeless, if predestined friends are concealed among our most brazen opponents, though they are still unknown even to themselves. Those two cities, then, have been woven together and mixed together in this age, until they are torn apart in the final judgment. Deliberating about what should be said, and divinely aided to whatever degree, I will narrate the rise, course, and proper ends of these cities, for the sake of the glory of the city of God.[3]

In the end, there will be no mixing between cities. The final judgment is a rupture into two discrete parts. But that is something we can only anticipate eschatologically. In this age, bounded by the *saeculum*, no clear distinctions are possible. As with Augustine's other anxieties about time, here too the idea of ascribing value to the present causes him problems. The scale is simply grander in the *City of God*. Present time is still at issue, but it is now the present *saeculum*, not the present instant. Yet the question remains: how can we determine anything about the present as we continue to live through the instability of a time without any fixed present? Our interpretation of the historical present is held in suspense. The distinctions shaping history will remain invisible until some eschatological limit-point. Looking back from such a late vantage is the sole way to establish claims about the present that would no longer be subject to revision. It is belatedness, a sense of deferral and retrospection, that ties all of these Augustinian reservations together.

City of God 2 begins and ends by reminding its readers that the Christian moral economy has a delayed payoff, given the difficulties involved in deciphering providence. Augustine acknowledges this as a difficult teaching (CD 2.2):

> This question occurred to me: why do divine benefits come even to irreligious and ungrateful people, and why do the hard facts of war likewise afflict religious and irreligious people equally? It is a diffuse question. Every day, in every way, both the gifts of God and the destruction of humanity fall upon both kinds of people indifferently, and many people are usually moved by this. I have been delayed on this for a while, so that I could answer the question that was necessary for the work I had undertaken.[4]

It rains, in other words, on the just and unjust alike. This is not a platitude. It is historical reality. The middle sections of *City of God* 2 reiterate the point that there is little correlation between the apparent piety of a people and their historical fate. Licentious polytheists won great battles; admirable monotheists lost them. If moral virtue and religious observance count for anything, it is not for gains in this world. Augustine goes so far as to say that justice is not a possible goal for states in any age. "There is no true justice," he writes (CD 2.21), "except in the republic whose founder and ruler is Christ—if we want to call this a republic, since we cannot deny that it is an affair of the people."[5] In a prior decade, the notion of a Christian *res publica* could have been appropriated in the name of a Christian emperor. Here, Augustine is applying it to the heavenly city wandering in uncertainty. Someone steals bread from their neighbor, but escapes punishment. A state invades its neighbor, but is not beaten back. And yet everything is ruled by providence. What we stumble upon here is not incongruity, but the limits of our understanding. Of the judgments decreed by hidden providence, Augustine writes (CD 2.23): "No one comprehends them, but no one can justly condemn them."[6] No one can condemn them because no one has a complete view of how all these events fit together.

This disjunction between moral acts and their consequences afflicts our present *saeculum*, but perhaps providence lets itself be seen more clearly in Scripture. The patriarchs were often rewarded for their obedience to God (though Job stands out as an exception). But that patriarchal standard is a foil, not a precedent, for our own condition. In our times, the most reprehensible among us are elevated to positions of power. This is the case under Christian regimes as well; even a pious emperor would not guarantee the future of Rome. Later in the *City of God*, Augustine treats Rome's fate with chilling nonchalance (CD 4.7): "Who knows the will of God concerning that affair?"[7] This would be cold comfort for fifth-century refugees desperate for a way back home. Is Augustine reducing political history to the dice-roll of chance? Not quite, since the God of hidden providence is not *Fortuna*, but the *rex saeculorum*. Christ is the ruler not just of this baffling age, but of the order of all ages (CD 4.33):

> God, who alone is the true God, is the author and giver of happiness. God gives earthly rule to both good and bad people, but not blindly, as if by chance; God is God, not Fortune. Rather, God does it according to the order of things and times, which is hidden to us but quite well-known to God. Still, it is not that God is subdued by this order of times and serves it. God rules it as a Lord and arranges it like a manager.[8]

Augustine upholds the divine right of rule without ascribing any inherent virtue to those who benefit from this right. The order is firm; fortune has no place. Yet the order is also hidden, so that we cannot interpret the fluctuations of political history in terms of merit. This *ordo rerum et temporum* calls us back to Augustine's *pulcherrimus ordo* (CF 13.35). It has authority over all, which lends it a justice and a beauty utterly beyond our grasp. Cloaked in mystery, this order resists our attempts to weaponize it for our own political purposes.

Even if the providential history can no longer be identified with *Fortuna*, it still strikes many as fatalistic. In *City of God 5*, the fate that Augustine has in mind is astrological. It has to do with the stars (O'Loughlin 1999). We might find ourselves gazing up at the night sky with the Manichaeans once more. By now, Augustine has grown more attached to the language of will, though this does not mean that he is defending a robust doctrine of free will. Instead, he wants to find a middle way between pure chance and observable influence (either of the stars or of moral merit) by pointing to a hidden chain of causality, in which even the human will finds itself entangled (CD 5.9). This chain is voluntary in a double sense: it incorporates human volition and is rooted in the divine will. Does it then remain a brand of divine fate? Augustine's response is again nonchalant (CD 5.8):

> There is no need to get worked up and fight a war of words with those who define fate not as the arrangement of the stars (e.g., when something is conceived or born or begun), but as the connection of all things and as the causal sequence (through which everything that happens happens), provided that they attribute this order of causes and this connection to the will and power of the supreme God, who is well and truly believed both to know everything before it happens and never to let anything go unordered...[9]

According to *City of God 5*, it is acceptable to acknowledge a causal order binding all things together, as long as we beat back the temptation to derive that order from the observable physical world. This temptation strikes whenever we claim too much on the basis of events both celestial and historical.

Politically speaking, this temptation reached fever pitch during the reign of Theodosius, which signaled to some Christians the dawn of a new era. By the time Augustine was composing *City of God 5*, though, he suspected Christians had overestimated the accuracy of their historical awareness. "It is far beyond our strength," he said (CD 5.21), "to discuss the hidden things of humankind or judge the merits of kingdoms with a quick inspection."[10] Yet the empire could look enticingly like a permanent home rather than temporary scaffolding. Augustine was not immune to this temptation, especially when he recalled the humility shown by Theodosius after Ambrose's rebuke over the massacre of the Thessalonians (McLynn 1999). Still, flattery is no match for providence (CD 5.26):

> These and similar works (which we could spend a long time recounting) were the good things Theodosius brought out of the temporal vapor of human heights and depths. The real wage for such work is eternal happiness, which God truly gives only to the pious. The other things of this life, whether the highest or the lowest—like the world itself, light, air, land, water, food, the human soul and body, sense, mind, life—all these God grants to both good and bad people. This also goes for great power of any kind, which God dispenses in God's governing of the times.[11]

The *tempora Christiana* were not a new golden age. Theodosius may or may not receive his reward in heaven, but even his humility before Ambrose does not tell us much about the structure of history. Augustine leaves us with a sense of what Henri-Irénée Marrou (1950: 40, 76–7) called historical ambivalence. Even when a comparatively well-behaved Christian becomes emperor, it means little. History's meaning is fixed yet shrouded. Our *saeculum* has been emptied of significance for us. For the divine, the order of things is beautiful; for us, it is overwhelming like the sublime.

The Joints of Time

The current age, emptied of illusory turning-points and specters of meaning, greets us as a homogeneous mess. Things continue to happen, but their value is opaque. Still, Augustine sets limits on this historical ambivalence. It does not extend all the way back to the beginning of time, because Scripture said something true about the past. Augustine already argued this concerning cosmic origins in the *Confessions*; in the *City of God*, he applies the same rationale to Scriptural accounts of humankind's past. Whereas human knowledge of historical meaning in this *saeculum* is severely limited, our awareness of long-lost events like Noah's flood or Abraham's sacrifice stands on surer ground, not because we are closer to those events, but because their meaning has been revealed in God's Word.

This newfound certainty allows Augustine to gain insight into the order of the ages which would otherwise be impossible. In *De Catechizandis Rudibus*, written between 399 and 405 CE as a manual for instructing new Christians, Augustine makes history hexaemeral. Six ages correspond to the six days of creation in Genesis, with the transition between each age marked by some great figure (CR 22: 121–78):

> Five ages of history have passed. The first ran from humankind's beginning (Adam, the first human ever made) to Noah, who made his ark during the flood. The second age is then from Noah to Abraham, chosen to be the Father of all the nations that imitate him in faith… The joints of these two ages are prominent only in the old books, but the joints of the remaining three ages are declared also in the gospel, when our Lord Jesus Christ's origin in the flesh is recounted. The third age is from Abraham to King David. The fourth is from David to the Babylonian captivity, when the people of God were exiled to Babylon. The fifth goes from that exile to the arrival of our Lord Jesus Christ. From his arrival onward, a sixth age is taking place.[12]

Note that these ages are connected by "joints." This is the same term (*articulus*) Augustine used to describe the "spring" from which temporal creation began in Genesis 2. Similar terminology is found in the *City of God*, especially from its tenth book onward. These "joints" link the ages together in a way that is normally hidden but exceptionally revealed by Scripture. Paying attention to Scripture, however, cannot increase our interpretive power concerning history as we live through it. This is what sets apart the sixth *saeculum*, stretching from the Incarnation to the eschaton.

Whereas *City of God* 10 revives the hexaemeral historiography of *De Catechizandis Rudibus*, *City of God* 11 focuses on the first day alone. Thanks to the *Confessions* and contrary to the Manichaeans, we know that this "day" did not occur in time, but marks the creation of temporality. Thanks to the *Literal Meaning of Genesis*, we also know that this "day" represents angelic consciousness (CD 11.7–9). This means Augustine is now ready to narrate the story of the two cities, one gazing upon God and the other turning away. The first to turn away are the fallen angels, but even their demonic fall befits the beautiful order of the ages (CD 11.18):

God would not create any angel or human God knew was going to be evil unless God knew equally how God would fit them in for the use of the good and adorn the order of the ages with certain antitheses, like the most beautiful song. Such antitheses, as they are called in an elaborate locution, are quite attractive. In plain Latin terms, we could call them oppositions or, to speak more clearly, counterpoints.[13]

Neither moralizing about history nor quibbling about the fallen angels can rob the cosmic order of its aesthetic equipoise. "The beauty of the age," adds Augustine, "is composed through the opposition of contraries." It is like a song, yet more than a song, because it is everything. It is "an eloquence of things," he says (CD 11.18), "not of words."[14] To appreciate this cosmological beauty would require a perspective no longer constrained by time, a consciousness unaffected by *distentio* and beyond the tense logic of past, present, and future. It would take a God (CD 11.21):

God's focus [*intentio*] does not pass over from thought to thought. In his bodiless awareness [*contuitus*], everything God knows is all there together at once. God knows the times, but not through any temporal kind of knowing. God sets temporal things in motion, but without any temporal movements.[15]

Confessions 11 and *City of God* 11 use the same language of *intentio* and *contuitus* for distinct but interwoven ends. In the former work, Augustine emphasizes time's effects on the soul. In the latter, his concerns are historical. In both, our *intentio* and *contuitus* waver and falter on the shores of *distentio*; for God, it is the opposite. Just as self-understanding arrives only belatedly in the *Confessions*, so in the *City of God* historical understanding arises long after the fact (if ever). "The universe of things is like a picture where dark colors have their place, too," writes Augustine (CD 11.23). "If someone could see it, it would be beautiful even with sinners."[16] For now, though, we struggle to see the whole picture, because we are part of that picture. Humility in judgment remains the order of the day.

Scripture alone narrates the history of the joints of time as they both separate and conjoin the various ages. This narrative is linear; it only plays out one way. We must overcome the ancient idea of cyclical time, which nevertheless remains tempting. After all, the seasons follow each other in a cycle, according to the motions of the planetary spheres. Augustine rejects this circular approach, since it threatens the security of true happiness (Löwith 1949: 163). What is the point of deferring eternal beatitude to the end of time, if time is just going to start back up again and hurl us back into the mire of history? Augustine further argues that the order of the *articuli temporis* must play out in linear fashion. The Fall, the flood, the fear and trembling on a mountain: all of these Scriptural events unfold in succession. The meaning of each depends on its position in the series. They are not repeatable. Of all these turning-points, the most sacrosanct in its uniqueness is the advent of Christ. "Christ died once for our sins," emphasizes Augustine (CD 12.14), foregrounding the *semel* ("once") in his sentence.[17]

Human history plays out on this same unidirectional plane, but there are no longer any obvious turning-points. History does not repeat itself, nor (despite Pinker) does it take the form of progress toward any better worldly life. Augustinian historiography resists the rush to posit world-historical moments of transformation, whereas Pinker (2018: 324) does just that when he explains the global situation by claiming "the Enlightenment is working." Such historical signposts are simplistic mirages hovering over the sands of time. Instead of hunting for objectively provable turning-points in history, Augustine suggests the heterogeneity that marked out the previous five ages of history has given way to the homogeneous duration of the sixth (Markus 1989: 20–3). We now live in an interim timeline. Mani's interim ran between the initial cataclysm and the final restoration of order; Augustine's interim spans from Christ's arrival to Christ's return. In order to find out what happened before this interim *saeculum*, Augustine must turn to Scripture. After *City of God* 13 and 14 take us from Adam's Fall to Noah's flood, Augustine picks up his historiographical pace in the post-diluvian era. Reminding his readers that the goal is to trace the development of the heavenly and earthly cities, he admits in *City of God* 16 that even in Scripture it is often unclear which characters belong to which city. After the flood, it becomes especially unclear whether the history of the heavenly city is continuous or fragmented (CD 16.1).

This lack of clarity continues down to the time of Abraham. The patriarch's long life somehow constitutes a singular event, which serves as a meaningful turning-point within the plot of Scripture.

Augustine explicitly frames the Abrahamic event as a joint (CD 16.12):

> Now then, let us look at the course of the city of God from that joint in time [*ab illo articulo temporis*] that occurred with father Abraham. From that joint, our knowledge of the city of God began to get clearer. There too we read more plainly the divine promises that we now see to have been fulfilled in Christ.[18]

From the wording of this passage, it is clear that Augustine is using *articulus temporis* to refer not to an age, but to a hinge upon which ages turn. Scripture serves as a user's manual for the mechanism of history, pointing out the location of a joint that would otherwise remain hidden. Knowing about these points of articulation proves invaluable for interpreting the meaning of the trials of Abraham and his successors. Joints make providence visible. In the story of Abraham, pious action tends to be met with earthly rewards, while impious action fares less well. This is the reverse image of the sick joke that is our own Christian era.

When Augustine gets to David at the end of *City of God* 16, he again draws our attention to the way Scripture can highlight the *articuli temporis*. Here his six-stage account of history is no longer hexaemeral, but instead modeled on an individual human life (CD 16.43):

> With David, there was made a certain joint [*articulus*]: the beginning, in a way, of the youth of the people of God. The adolescence of humankind, if you will, lasted from Abraham down to David. The evangelist Matthew did not recount these generations in vain. He attributed forty such generations to this first interval (from Abraham to David). From adolescence, then, humankind gained the ability to generate. And so the count of generations begins with Abraham, who was made the father of peoples when he received his name change. Before him, then, the people of God were in their childhood (from Noah to Abraham). This is when language (Hebrew, that is) was discovered. People begin to speak in childhood, after all, once infancy is over. Infancy, of course, means inability to speak. Our forgetfulness submerges this first stage of life, just as the first stage of humankind was destroyed by the flood. How many people could there be who can recall their infancy?[19]

Augustine introduces his six-age analogy in reverse. Starting with the strength of youth (from David onward), he moves back through the reproductive power of adolescence (from Abraham to David), past the linguistic development of childhood (from Noah to Abraham), and into the oblivion of infancy (from Adam to Noah). Note that this periodization is explicitly retrospective. It is as if the outline of humankind's history cannot be grasped until we have reached the end of history, just like the meaning of an individual's life can only be summed up after they are dead.

Augustine reverts to his model of the hexaemeron in the climactic lines of the *City of God*. "If we calculate the number of the ages as if they were days," he writes (CD 22.30), "according to the joints of time [*articulos temporis*] that Scripture seems to make clear, then there will obviously appear to be a Sabbath, since that is the seventh day."[20] Everything begins with Adam. Noah is the hinge between the first and second age; Abraham between the second and third; David between the third and fourth; the Babylonian exile between the fourth and fifth; Christ between the fifth and sixth. Each of these periods corresponds to the aforementioned stages of life: in addition to infancy, childhood, adolescence, and youth, there is entry into adulthood (leading up to the Incarnation) and then the old age of the world (after Christ). The joint connecting this sixth age of senescence to a seventh would therefore be the eschaton. That suits the structure of *City of God* 22, which acquaints us with the eschatological endpoint of all things. The length of the *senectus mundi*, meanwhile, is immeasurable. The sixth age is happening now, but it cannot be counted up in terms of generations (CD 22.30). It is not for us to know the times (Acts 1:7), at least until the sun has set on the sixth day.

The poet Guy Davenport (1981: 30) once translated a fragment of Heraclitus as follows: "Joints are and are not parts of the body. They cooperate through opposition, and make a harmony of separate forces. Wholeness arises from distinct particulars; distinct particulars occur in wholeness." Something like this understanding of joints helps us get at what Augustine is doing with the *articuli temporis*. When it comes to making sense of history, we feel a need to posit turning-points or hinges around which all other events revolve and from which they gain their significance. We usually do so belatedly, after the fact. Even then, determining which past event deserves to be elevated above the rest is no easy task. But how would we spin stories without selectivity? Without turning-points, we would be left with an endless onslaught of empty, homogeneous events. There would be no story to tell.

Perhaps, like Aristotle's points on a line, the joints of history are merely retrospective markers we posit in order to arrive at a manageable picture. They may not really be there in the past, just like a point has no place within a pure continuum. Like the joints of Heraclitus, they both are and are not part of the whole they articulate. Augustine affixes these *articuli* to Scripture. By doing so, he closes off the possibility of their appearance once the narrative of Scripture has drawn to a close (Markus 1989: 43). After the gospel, which marks out the joint that is the event of Christ, there is only the dead calm of the *saeculum*. To posit turning-points after this is unadvisable. Not even the Sack of Rome counts as a new hinge in history. In the *City of God*, Augustine is questioning our capacity to interpret history as we live through it in this interim *saeculum*. "Do not pronounce judgment before the time," advises Paul (1 Cor. 4:5). Applying this maxim to history, we could say that the significance of the present age, in its full articulation, will only become clear at the end of time. Until that point, Augustine's approach to historical meaning should remind us of another Heraclitean fragment, rendered again by Davenport (1981: 27): "Good days and bad days, says Hesiod, forgetting that all days are alike."

Eschatological Belatedness

Augustine's joints of time and empty *saeculum* indicate that his approach to historical meaning is eschatological. This does not mean he anticipated an imminent apocalypse (Markus 1989: 19–20). He offers deferred eschatology, emphasizing the interminable delay lying between our supposed present and the end of time. Christ's return is bound to strike us as arriving a bit late. Eschatological belatedness afflicts history, then, just as psychological belatedness afflicts the individual life. From *Confessions* 4, we learned that it was incarnate experience or the sense of the flesh that was late (*tardus*). This need not mean that the body (*corpus*) is to blame for belatedness, since flesh (*caro*) is for Augustine a moral category not synonymous with embodiment. He emphasizes this point in *City of God* 13, where the scope of history takes us from the beginning of death (as the wages of Adam's sin) to the defeat of death in the general resurrection. Only in that final transformation will the body overcome belatedness (CD 13.20):

> Spirit that serves flesh is not unfittingly called fleshly. Likewise, flesh that serves spirit is rightly called spiritual, but not because it is converted into spirit. No one thinks that when they read: "It is sown an ensouled body, it will rise a spiritual body." Rather, such flesh is called spiritual because it is subdued by the spirit. It obeys spirit with a supreme and surprising ease, so that the most secure will of indissoluble immortality is fulfilled. Such flesh has lost all sense of trouble, all decay, all belatedness [*tarditas*].[21]

There is a remedy for belatedness, but we do not have it yet. Baptism does not quicken our pace (CD 13.23). Presuming baptism to have altered our experience of time would be prideful self-deception. Better, Augustine thinks, to wait on the absolute future. In the meantime, the wisest move would be to accept that we are largely passive before the force of time. There remains a disjunctive delay between what we think we wish to do and what we actually do (CD 14.15). To rush ahead in our activity would be to act as if we were masters of history. This is one way of interpreting Augustine's two cities: the one seeking to control time is motivated by love of self; the one awaiting future grace is motivated by love of God (CD 14.28). The strange thing is that the boundaries of these cities do not appear to us as fixed across time. They seem to be shifting. Our awareness of our own communities is just as provisional as our awareness of ourselves.

Citizenship in either city is determined eschatologically, with some notable exceptions. Enoch, who lived between the *articuli* of Adam and Noah, was somehow carried off to God without having to die (Gen. 5:21-4). But if Enoch can be directly translated into some heavenly realm, why must we wait so long? Heading off such worries, Augustine is quick to label Enoch an exceptional case (CD 15.24):

> The translation of Enoch has prefigured the deferral [*dilatio*] of our own dedication [to God]. To be sure, this was done in Christ, our head, who rose to die no more, and was also translated.

Yet another dedication remained for the universal house that has Christ as a foundation. This dedication is deferred until the end [*differtur in finem*], when all will be resurrected to die no more.[22]

Augustine is emphatic about the delay between our age and this dedication of the house of Christ. To assume we are already within the walls of the divine house would be premature. The rest of the heavenly city must await eschatological confirmation, precisely in the way that Enoch did not. For now, residents of both cities are caught up in the same historical net, to borrow Augustine's analogy from *City of God* 18. Caught fish that we are, we wait to be sorted out once ashore. Upon that shore, the sun of justice will shine on all, dividing up that which is intermingled. In this era, however, not even the visible institution of the church can distinguish those who have been chosen from those who have not. Augustine sums up the situation (CD 18.49):

Many of the rejected are mixed in with good people. Both are gathered up in the Church, as if it were a net. Both swim in the sea of this world, indiscriminately caught in the same net. But when they arrive at the shore, the evil will be separated out from the good. And God will be all in all in the good, as if in God's temple.[23]

The dedication of the house of God occurs on that eschatological shore. Until then, we are caught writhing about in history's tangled rigging. But when will we be set free? Augustine returns again to Acts 1:7-8 (CD 18.1): "It is not for you to know the times that the Father, in His power, put in place." Augustine holds contemporary preachers of apocalyptic imminence to be in violation of this Scriptural precept (CD 18.53).

Attempts to render the eschaton imminent, from wild-eyed apocalyptic preaching to Pinker's promise of enlightenment now, erroneously treat the temporal as if it had become eternal. Augustine was awakened to this truth with the death of his friend in Thagaste. In the *City of God*, he applies this truth to the two possible destinies of human life. To seek the goal of this life in the present is to assume that salvation consists in some present state, be it pleasure or virtue or survival. Real salvation, however, consists in true happiness, which can only be guaranteed in timeless eternity. Beatific peace is not a possession to be claimed in advance, but a gift to be awaited. "Just as we are saved by hope, so are we blessed by hope," writes Augustine (CD 19.4). "Just as we do not have a grip on salvation at present, so we do not yet have a grip on blessedness. Rather, we are waiting on the future, and we are doing this patiently."[24] Hope should not be cheapened into sham-certainty. What is called for is *sollicitudo*: a fruitful anxiety over the lack of certainty concerning our fate. This sense of being shaken afflicts everyone (CD 19.10):

> Even the saints, even those who faithfully worship the one true and highest God, have not been made secure from deception and manifold temptation. But in this place of weakness, in these malicious days, such disturbance is not useless. Its usefulness is to make us seek with a more fervent desire that security where peace is fullest and most certain.[25]

We need to be shaken up if we are to be shaken out of our self-delusions about life in time. To seek certainty too soon or to dream that our age is the best one possible would be, for Augustine, to project a false sense of peace upon a world that is undergoing transformation. "This is how pride perversely imitates God," writes Augustine (CD 19.12). "It hates to share equality under God with its peers, but it wants to install its own domination over them instead of God's. So it hates God's just peace and loves its own unjust peace."[26] The *pax Romana* or Pinker's science might have their uses, but neither amounts to peace in its truest sense. For that, we would have to glimpse the beautiful order of the ages, which is what always eludes us. "The peace of all things," says Augustine (CD 19.13):

> is the tranquility of order. Order is the arrangement of all things, equal and unequal, which assigns to each its place. So the miserable, who are absolutely not at peace insofar as they are miserable, lack this tranquility of order where there is no disturbance. But still, since they are deservedly and justly miserable, they cannot be outside of the order, even in their misery. To be sure, they are not joined together with the blessed, but nevertheless they are separated from the blessed according to the law of order.[27]

Here cosmology and ethics collide. Justice is not a set of legal proceedings, but the right ordering of things. Happiness and peace are not aims of civil law, but eschatological possibilities. We do not know the order of the times. But time will end. The order of things will be revealed to us. Until then, we must learn to be patient.

The most damnable temptation is our desire to judge the heavenly from the earthly city in advance. If anything should be final, it is this judgment. The event of the final judgment serves as the last hinge of historical time. Through it, the whole divine order will become apparent in retrospect. In an unthinkable instant, the sublime mess of the *saeculum* will be cleaned up and laid bare for all to see. Only then will there be a correlation between what we deserve and what we get. Augustine puts it bluntly (CD 20.1): "The day when there will be no place for ignorant whining about why the unjust are happy while the just are unhappy is most properly called the day of judgment. Only then will there appear true and full happiness for all who are good, with deservedly supreme unhappiness for those who are evil."[28]

From a God's eye view, of course, the decision between good and evil has already been made. An eternal deity will not make a spur of the moment judgment at the end of time; God is always timelessly judging. But the content of that judgment has not yet been revealed. As long as we stay entangled in the net of the *saeculum*, we have difficulty telling fish from fish. Even those baptized within the walls of the Church may fall away before the end: it should not bother us that the devil often seduces even those who have already been reborn in Christ and are walking the paths of God. "The Lord knows who are His" (CD 20.7; 2 Tim. 2:19). No one from that group is seduced into eternal damnation by the devil. The Lord knows them as God: nothing, not even the future, is concealed from Him. He does not know them like people know other people. We see other people when they are present (if indeed we see them, since we do not see their hearts). But we do not see what they are going to be like later, just as we do not even see what we ourselves are going to be like later.[29]

In the moment, we are unable to vet anyone's eschatological citizenship documents. God alone knows who belongs in which city. Our documents have been drafted, in other words, but they remain illegible to us. Rev. 20:12 refers to books of death and life: "I saw the dead, great and small, standing before the throne, and books were opened. Also another book was opened, the book of life. And the dead were judged according to their works, as recorded in the books." The content of these volumes will become apparent only at the final judgment. As Augustine describes it (CD 20.14):

> we should understand that there will be a certain divine force that will make it so that everyone's works, whether good or bad, will all be called back into their memories. With astonishing speed, these works will be sorted out via a mental intuition. Knowledge will accuse or excuse them according to conscience. In this way, each and every person will be judged simultaneously. No wonder, then, this divine force has received the name "book." In it, whatever is recalled through its effectivity is, in a way, "read."[30]

Like our citizenship documents, the books of the dead are closed to us. Their ink is too faded to read. But that does not make their pages blank. For Augustine, what is needed to interpret someone's life is not a more well-rounded human perspective, but a divine force. Nothing but this could navigate the depths of human memory.

If the many books of the dead collapse temporally disordered human lives into one condemnable lump, the sole book of life is the atemporal decision of the divine, standing beyond all disorder. The purpose of that book is not to be read by God, but to be opened up for us at the end (CD 20.15):

> But this book does not remind God, as if God would otherwise forget and be mistaken. Instead, this book signifies the predestination of those whom God is going to give eternal life. It is not that God is ignorant of them and needs to read this book to learn about them. Rather, God's foreknowledge of them, which cannot be mistaken, is this book of life.

That they have been written in this book means they have been known in advance.[31] With its fixed but unreadable text, the book of life remains both decisive for us and unknown to us. Augustine's reading of Revelation affirms the priority of divine decision while resisting the hubristic supposition that we can write ourselves into the book of life before the time. We cannot say that those who are now doing well deserve it; nor can we say that those who suffer deserve it. Things are not becoming more or less just, as far as we can tell, in this interim *saeculum*. The relation between our *saeculum* and the eschaton is not one of slowly progressing legibility. It is an unimaginable rupture. The revelation of the distance between the just and the unjust will be the advent of heterogeneity finally destroying the empty homogeneity of time. Until then, the pages of history might as well be blank.

All of this might sound pessimistic. Yet, even as those who appear to be just might turn out to be unjust, the same could be true of those who seem irredeemable. They could re-enter the fold sometime between today and the eschaton. That is why they must be prayed for rather than rooted out. Of the Church, Augustine writes (CD 21.24):

> For now, it prays for those it holds to be enemies, since it is the time of fruitful repentance. Why would it pray for them at all, if not so that, as the Apostle says, "God might give them repentance so they are rescued from the snares of the devil, who was holding them captive on account of their own wills?" [2 Tim. 2:25–6] Lastly, if the church were so certain that it knew who in this life was predestined to go into eternal fire with the devil, it would pray neither for them nor for the devil. But since it is certain about no one, to this extent the church prays for all its embodied enemies. Still, its prayers are not always heard. The church's prayers for its enemies are only heard when those who are opposed to the church are nevertheless predestined, so that the church's prayers on their behalf are heard and they are made children of the church.[32]

Augustine sets the stability of the divine decision alongside our inability to take hold of that stability for ourselves. These might strike us as competing claims. On the one hand, Augustine is telling us to pray for outsiders, since we do not know who will turn out to be on the inside in the end. On the other hand, he is saying that our prayers will not be heard if God has not already chosen those outsiders. The work of human hands seems to bristle against the timeless decision of the divine. Augustine, however, sees no competition between God and humankind. The *saeculum* greets us as emptied of meaning not because there really is no order, but because the order is concealed. Justice strikes us as impossible not because it is impossible, but because it is impossible for us to fully grasp it. Providence is kept hidden, but God is still provident. We cannot see grace descend like a dove, yet it counts for everything. What Augustine is doing here is thinking his way through the relationship between a timeless decision and lives lived in time.

Conclusion

In *Enlightenment Now*, the cornerstone of Pinker's argument was the quantifiable progress of human history over time. "What is progress?" he asks in one memorable passage (Pinker 2018: 51). "You might think that the question is so subjective and culturally relative as to be forever unanswerable. In fact, it's one of the easier questions to answer." Pinker (2018: 51) continues:

> Most people agree that life is better than death. Health is better than sickness. Sustenance is better than hunger. Abundance is better than poverty. Peace is better than war. Safety is better than danger. Freedom is better than tyranny. Equal rights are better than bigotry and discrimination. Literacy is better than illiteracy. Knowledge is better than ignorance. Intelligence is better than dull-wittedness. Happiness is better than misery. Opportunities to enjoy family, friends, culture, and nature are better than drudgery and monotony.

But how are we to define knowledge or happiness or any of these other load-bearing terms? How can we interpret the term "better" in such a way that it can account for all these dichotomies? For Pinker, prattling questions like these rattle the pessimistic intelligentsia and few others. All of the above qualities, he argues (Pinker 2018: 51), "can be measured. If they have increased over time, that is progress." Pinker's language of measurement lends itself to graphic representation. Let the x axis stand for time; let the y axis stand for human flourishing. Now draw a line that, albeit imperfectly, trends diagonally upward and to the right. This is Pinker's theology of history.

Augustine's approach to history runs counter to Pinker's at almost every turn. This is not because he courts regression over progress, but because he resists the urge to uncover some underlying, quantifiable logic within history. Löwith was right to argue that modern linear time is reminiscent of Augustinian eschatological time, but Augustine was not guilty of selling progress narratives. The joints of time articulating history were revealed in Scripture, but they cannot be found in our interim *saeculum*. What matters, for Augustine, is the beginning and the end: Genesis and Revelation. "What changes for better or worse in the intervening time will not be judged," he wrote (CD 17.4). "What will be judged is what will be found at the very end. That is why it was said: 'Whoever will have persevered until the end will be saved.'"[33] The words of Mt. 24:13 convey the inscrutable logic of salvation history.

For Pinker, "what changes for better or worse" in our statistical estimation counts for everything. It is what makes the present era special. For Augustine, however, judging things before the end merely reveals to us how uncomfortable we are with our own temporal situation. Enlightenment is not rational mastery of the universe, but graceful illumination shining out from God. Enlightenment is held in reserve for the seventh day of hexaemeral historiography: the eschatological Sabbath (CD 22.30). With that final point of articulation, the six-day schema will both culminate and evaporate. Humankind will draw as near as it can to timelessness, with the citizens of the heavenly city entering into the heaven of heavens. To claim a timeless perspective now, though, is to perversely imitate God. It is pride to ignore the belatedness afflicting our temporal lives. Belatedness, then, names the difference between our perspective and God's. We are out of step not only with the present instant of time, but also with the present age of history. Caught up in the order of times, we know not what they mean. Instead, we face the meaningless barrage of events making up our *saeculum*. Meaning, order, and closure will arrive late. The times will settle into place when there is no longer any time. The song will be appreciated once it has been sung.

4

Do Not Live in the Now

A Critique of Mindfulness

Introduction

A 2017 article written by Jen Christensen for CNN's health site argues that present-minded living is the key to wellness (Christensen 2017). Titled "Meaningful Mindfulness: How It Could Help You Be Happier, Healthier, and More Successful," the piece rests upon the insights of figures as varied as the Dalai Lama, Lady Gaga, and Kobe Bryant. Optimism regarding our ability to transform our experience of time abounds. Christensen's article even includes a subheading that reads: "Making Mindfulness Great Again." Pop-psychological advice abounds, sometimes verging on unintentional comedy, such as the following line from Richard Davidson of the University of Wisconsin's Center for Healthy Minds. "Suffering," he informs us, "is becoming increasingly recognized as a serious problem." More helpful is the definition of mindfulness offered to CNN by Jon Kabat-Zinn of the Center for Mindfulness at the University of Massachusetts: mindfulness consists in "paying attention on purpose, in the present moment, non-judgmentally."

In works straddling the line between academic research and self-help literature, Kabat-Zinn and others have furthered detailed their mindfulness programs. It helps to glaze a layer of scientific credibility over the advice on offer. The clinical psychologist Mark Williams and the biochemist Danny Penman, for example, used their expertise to craft a step-by-step strategy for attaining mental tranquility. Their book, *Mindfulness: An Eight-Week Plan for Finding Peace in a Frantic World*, featuring a foreword by Kabat-Zinn, adds to the consensus among mindfulness experts that present-mindedness undergirds the successful life. For Williams and Penman (2011: 200), mindfulness meditation allows us to anchor ourselves "back in the present moment," as if we were once rooted in the present and slipped away into the past or the future by mistake. The authors quote Einstein to justify their advice to live in the present, although the quotation they use has more to do with compassion than with relativistic theories of time (Williams and Penman 2011: 210).

All of this present-mindedness results in some surprisingly bold rejections of the past and future. Mindfulness meditation, promise Williams and Penman (2011: 11), will reveal to us the tautological truth that memories are memories and, as a consequence, "are like propaganda; *they are not real*. They are not *you*" (original emphasis). A focus on the present comes at the cost of memory. Back in *Confessions* 10, however, Augustine showed us that *memoria* could never be so easily erased from time-consciousness. On Augustinian terms, it would be safer to say that we are indeed our memories, as disturbing as that fact might be. Whereas Augustine sought to diminish the privilege of the present for the sake of past memories and an eschatological future, mindfulness literature does the opposite. The present expands outward, colonizing the past and future in the name of therapeutic salvation. While Williams and Penman are most concerned by the power of the past, their peer Richard Sears (also a clinical psychologist) emphasizes the danger of planning for the future. For Sears (2014: 27), our goal should be to practice "being in each now moment," even though the "future that we long for, or fear, will be just another now." As far as Sears (2014: 27) is concerned, the art of mindfulness consists in "starting fresh again in every moment, moment after moment." Just like the CNN article, then, the advice offered by figures like Kabat-Zinn, Sears, Williams, and Penman is rooted in the present-centric, momentary account of time they all share. The implication is that, by focusing on the present moment, we can free ourselves from enchainment to past regrets and future fears, thereby attaining a salutary new level of mental stability.

These self-help books and publicity pieces speak to an ongoing interest in the connection between trauma and the present.

Exemplary is the work of Ellen Langer, who markets mindfulness to twenty-first-century business people. As Langer (2017: 4) advertises, mindfulness means "the process of actively noticing new things. When you do that, it puts you in the present." Like many others, Langer grounds her insights in both modern medicine and traditional wisdom. The preferred form of traditional wisdom is usually Buddhist thought. Fittingly, the CNN article features a clip of the Dalai Lama extolling the virtues of meditation. Any meaningful distinctions between his meditative experience and the mindfulness being marketed are, for the most part, elided. Yet Buddhism is not the sole ancient parallel for the modern mindfulness movement.

More relevant to the topic of Augustinian temporality would be the Stoicism of Mediterranean antiquity, which also preached present-minded focus. The Stoics, by no means relegated to the classical world, have seen a resurgence. The work of Pierre Hadot has done much to keep alive the ideal of present-minded attentiveness. One of his favorite lines is drawn from Marcus Aurelius' *Meditations* (4.49): "Lucky am I that, though this has befallen me, yet am I still unhurt, neither crushed by the present nor dreading the future." The sentiment may be admirable, but it is far from Augustinian. Hadot's approach was memorialized in a 2001 series of interviews conducted by Arnold Davidson and Jeannie Carlier, published in 2011 as *The Present Alone Is Our Happiness*. There, responding to a question about the attraction of ancient philosophy, Hadot (2009: 162) speaks of "the infinite value of the present moment" stripped bare of past and future considerations. This is not so much a mathematical instant lacking width as a full-bodied present. While he attributes the wisdom of present-mindedness to the Stoics (alongside the Epicureans), Hadot also recounts a half-remembered anecdote concerning the sixteenth-century Jesuit Aloysius Gonzaga, supposedly found somewhere in the works of the twentieth-century French mystic Charles Péguy. When he was still a child playing a game with friends, Gonzaga was asked what he would do if told he had one hour to live. His answer was that he would play on. According to Hadot, Marcus Aurelius would have agreed.

Augustine, however, preferred prayer in his final hours. He recited psalms of lamentation as the Vandals amassed near the gates of Hippo. Antiquity offered different strategies for facing up to death. Given the intimate relationship between temporality and mortality, it is no surprise that we find embedded in these different strategies equally distinct approaches to time. Augustine's take on temporal experience can be described as anti-mindfulness, which will have consequences for his approach to both psychology and politics.

Stoic Mindfulness

In 2012, the Modern Stoicism movement held its first official Stoic Week at Exeter University. The plan was for a small group of students to live like ancient Stoics, if only for seven days. It proved so popular that the number of participants ballooned. According to the Modern Stoicism site, about 150 people joined in the fun, resulting in a "10% reduction in negative emotions over the course of the week." Since 2012, at least 20,000 people have enjoyed this adventure in mindfulness. Setting aside the question of whether or not a quantitative metric of negative emotions is acceptable on Augustinian grounds, we should start by asking: what is it about ancient Stoicism that so appeals to the modern mind? It is probably not the Stoics' interest in fate or their fire-centric cosmology that attracts undergraduates and professionals in search of life-coaching. The therapeutic aspect of Stoicism, rather than Stoic physics or ethics, attracts the most attention.

Where the axes of temporality and therapy meet in Stoicism, we find present-mindedness. Some Stoics emphasize the present more or less than others, of course. In his first-century *Discourses*, for example, Epictetus does not dwell upon the philosophy of time, preferring instead to cultivate a non-judgmental attitude, which is also a crucial component of Kabat-Zinn's definition of mindfulness. When the mind is presented with some current event, it should not rush to judgment about its moral import. Instead, we must let the present impression be what it is: nothing but an impression, delivering perceptual content without any attached value judgments. If, for example, you hear that your mother has been thrown in jail, you should not immediately leap to the conclusion that this is an evil. According to Epictetus' *Discourses* 3.8.1–5 (2014: 159–60), the distinction between good and evil only enters the scene later, once you begin to process this information by grieving it (which is evil) or bearing it (which is good). The goal of philosophical instruction, for Epictetus, was to internalize these facts of Stoic teaching so intimately that their "truth and implications would be as obvious" to the student as are "self-evident matters of empirical fact" (Long 2002: 106).

Augustine would applaud an ethos of humility in the face of morally obscure situations. Given his account of temporal experience as belatedness, however, he would be skeptical of the idea that we retain sovereignty over impressions as they appear to us. For Epictetus (2014: 279), however, the only thing that matters is "what lies within our power," which is "the decision of our will." With his language of *prohairesis*, he embeds autonomous choice at the heart of his teachings. For some readers (Long 2002: 229–30), this leads to disharmony between the Stoic account of volition and the Stoic cosmology of fate. Looked at naturalistically, all relationships of cause and effect can be traced back to Zeus, the "universal causal agent" (Long 2002: 229). Looked at from the perspective of the willing agent, autonomous choice reigns, even if the goal of the Stoic sage is to freely choose that which the universal causal agent would have the sage choose regardless. Zeus' destiny returns to swallow freedom back up into fate.

Despite this tension between Stoic ethics and Stoic physics, it remains obvious that, for Epictetus (2014: 280), sovereign volition wields the "power to deal with impressions." This is what lies within our power; this is what depends on us. Presumably, the decision to refrain from applying a value judgment to an event would take place in an instant. But here, in the context of Epictetus' advice, we seldom find the problem of time treated with any depth. As far as Stoic sovereignty in the face of present impressions is concerned, "what is present" is not the present time in any rigorous sense. It is a current event; it is news.

The connection between a non-judgmental attitude and the present time proper is thrown into bolder belief by Marcus Aurelius in his second-century *Meditations*. It is no surprise that Marcus is one of Hadot's favorite figures to discuss when praising present-mindedness. Hadot (2009: 172) lauds the emperor's record as a ruler (spotty though it was for Christians under his watch) and credits his writings with "extraordinary lucidity" and a "precious" character.

According to Hadot (2009: 166), it is Marcus who best teaches us that the present "puts us in touch with the whole cosmos." To the Epicureans Hadot attributes a similar present-mindedness, although it is motivated more by hedonism than rationalism. The Epicurean privileges present pleasure, whereas the Stoic privileges present prudence as the practical wisdom that becomes possible when we fully invest ourselves in whatever our current activity happens to be. Hadot (2009: 164) finds an echo of the Epicurean vision in Rousseau's 1778 *Reveries of a Solitary Walker*, with his call to be fully present in the face of sublime nature. Goethe's poem "The Rule of Life" cuts straight to the heart of the matter (Hadot 2009: 164): "Do not let the past worry you." "Rejoice in the present." "Abandon the future to God." Even the phrase "the present alone is our happiness" was taken by Hadot from Goethe's *Faust II* (Hadot 2009: 164). The problem with this quotation, as Hadot (2009: 165) admits, is that Faust's obsession with the present moment is bound to the joy he feels while in the presence of his lover Helen. This means that Faust falls short of appreciating the fact that, as Marcus Aurelius expressed so vividly, each instant bears infinite value. This is true not just of happy moments, but of the moment in general as the core of temporal existence. In the wake of Goethe, figures as diverse as Rosa Luxemburg, Jean-Paul Sartre, and Aleksandr Solzhenitsyn incorporated mindfulness into their philosophical and political ways of life. In the end, however, Hadot always circles back to Marcus Aurelius and the Stoic form of rational present-mindedness, which he treasures more than the hedonistic presentism of the Epicureans.

In *Meditations* 2, Marcus tells us why we should not fear mortality. Death does not rob us of a possible future, because such a future does not exist. This makes the future unlike the present, which does exist. It is the sole locus of our being in time. According to *Meditations* 2.14:

> For the present time is of equal duration for all, while that which we lose is not ours; and consequently what is parted with is obviously a mere moment. No man can part with either the past or the future. For how can a man be deprived of what he does not possess?

A few lines later in *Meditations* 2.14 we find: "For it is but the present that a man can be deprived of, if, as is the fact, it is this alone that he has, and what he has not a man cannot part with." As if that were not clear enough, Marcus returns to the point in *Meditations* 3.10: "Remember withal that it is only this present, a moment of time, that a man lives: all the rest either has been lived or may never be." The key to happiness is first to accept that our life is constrained to the present moment, then to become content with whatever has been allotted to us in that moment.

If everything depends upon our focus on this present moment, must the present moment be a real thing upon which we could focus? Stoic present-mindedness might collapse into a realist stance about the present as the cornerstone of temporality. In that case, we would have to assign to the Stoics their own brand of momentariness, according to which the timeline is broken up into discrete chunks or time-atoms. This was a live option in Buddhist thought; perhaps it was also thinkable for ancient Mediterranean philosophers. The Epicureans, for example, reduced the spatial universe to atoms. Maybe they did the same for time. The evidence here is suggestive, though inconclusive. In *De Rerum Natura* (4.749–817), dating to the first century BCE, the Epicurean Lucretius writes of time as if it were made up of moments, at least in certain passages. Unfortunately, in other passages, he suggests that time is not a fundamental component of the universe, which might undermine the sense that his time-atoms are fully real.

Stoic discussions of the present time, meanwhile, tend to remain more therapeutic than cosmological. As Hadot (2009: 163) put it, the goal was to unburden ourselves of the "weight of the past" and free our minds from "fear of the future." Nevertheless, Marcus' language verges in the direction of atomism. Instead of the *atomos*, Marcus in his *Meditations* (2.14; 3.10; 4.48) writes of the *akariaion*. Both *atomos* and *akariaion* mean something akin to "uncuttable," though they opt for different cutting verbs. Both also imply that at some level of reality there exist atoms of time that are no longer divisible. This, of course, is what Augustine found to be impossible in *Confessions* 11. The obvious defense that could be offered by a Stoic apologist would be to say that Marcus is referring to psychological temporality, which matters most in therapeutic and ethical contexts. That is a fair defense, except for the fact that, as Hadot (2001: 90) showed in his *Inner Citadel*, one of the key attractions of Stoic philosophy was that all of its components were engineered to hang together. Logic, ethics, and physics were three faces of the same underlying truth. The philosopher James Warren (2002: 193) laid this down in the clearest of terms: "it is never the case that the ethical theories of ancient philosophers can be divorced entirely from the metaphysical and theological aspects of their respective systems." The spiritual exercises promoted by ancient Stoics were therapeutic in their goal, but cosmological in their root. They were logical, ethical, and physical all at once. As a result, in order for present-minded mindfulness to contribute to our mental health, there must be a real present. Otherwise, we would be not only misguided, but even self-contradictory.

Augustine and Stoicism

In many of his writings, Augustine sets himself against the Stoics, resisting especially any false hope for emotional *apatheia* or impassibility (CD 19.4; Boersma 2017). Christians must feel the suffering of existence, even if they are never to accuse God of being the author of that suffering. And yet, as Sarah Byers (2013) has shown, there are Stoic resonances in Augustine. For the most part, those resonances have to do with Augustine's account of how perception relates to volition. Recall here the non-judgmental quality of Stoic mindfulness, according to which we must not move too quickly from apparent impressions to moral judgments. On this Augustine and the Stoics are roughly in agreement. They arrive at similar (though not identical) positions, but not for the same reasons.

According to Byers (2013: 217), what Augustine means by *voluntas* or will is akin to what the Stoics mean by *hormē* or impulse. Drawing on a range of sources, Byers demonstrates that Augustinian will is (in a general sense) an impetus to action and (in a more restricted sense) the efficient cause of action in rational beings. Augustine further treats *voluntates* as "dispositions" or dispositional grounds for action, which are subtly related to another kind of impetus, the *appetitus* or "occurrent" impulse to perform an action (Byers 2013: 218–21). Strictly speaking, then, a "will" or *voluntas* is not a discrete decision to choose one thing over another, but an underlying disposition to pursue a particular class of objects (Byers 2013: 220). Human volition is therefore multilayered. Instead of existing in some neutral state, where we might freely choose one thing over against another (like, say, good over against evil), we already find ourselves inhabiting a volitional disposition which orients our desire toward certain kinds of objects. Living in the wake of Adam's original sin, regrettably, we tend to find ourselves already desiring objects less worthy of our love than is the divine. However, on Byers' account, this does not erase our agency, since there is still the possibility of an *appetitus*: an occurrent impulse which might stand a chance of overcoming our current disposition and orienting us toward a new, better class of objects.

One challenge for Byers is the fact that Augustine seldom sticks to this neat distinction between *appetitus* and *voluntas*. Often, he simply repeats the term *voluntas*, even though he is describing a complex series of volitional situations, rather than just one disposition (CD 14.11; Byers 2013: 222). The diligent reader must be skilled in the subtleties of Stoicism in order to pry Augustine's quasi-Stoic theory of volition out of his unsystematic prose. While Byers' argument is compelling, the fact that Augustine's own vocabulary of *voluntas* resists systematization should give us pause. It is possible that volition remained for him a curious mix of dispositional and occurrent aspects (to preserve Byers' terminology), never quite letting itself be sorted out into proper Stoic categories. Adopting an unsystematic interpretation of Augustinian willing would also better correspond to the messiness of Augustinian temporality. *Distentio* and belatedness are not so much systematic keywords as names of problems resistant to philosophical systematization. Perhaps the same is true of *voluntas*.

Bringing temporality and volition into closer conversation will require us to leave a gap between Stoic moral agency and Augustinian psychology. Even if we import Byers' distinction between dispositional and occurrent impulses into Augustine, his writings still resist the rhetoric of free will found in some Stoics. In *Discourses* 4.1 (2014: 217–37), Epictetus tells us that even if the universe quakes at the nod of Zeus, we remain free when dealing with the impressions within us. Disposition is not destiny, since occurrent impulses can occasion discrete acts of psychological sovereignty. If these discrete acts occur in succession, Epictetus suggests in *Discourses* 1.4 (2014: 12) that "progress" becomes possible. Augustine, however, aims to further circumscribe free will's sphere of influence. His counsel of humility, moreover, is not predicated on the idea that every event is value-neutral in itself. Rather, there is a secret logic to things, even though we have no access to that logic. To return to the example of grieving a dead loved one: the reason why it is unadvisable to obsess over one's grief is not because it is wrong to grieve, but because our obsession betrays our underlying presumption to know the right time for life to begin or end. Attachment to the world of fleeting things finds its cure not in cold *apatheia*, but in the rejection of pride and the dual embrace of grace and lamentation (CD 9.5).

The more noticeable gap between Augustine and the Stoics is the chasm dividing their treatments of temporality. We search Augustine's works in vain for a Stoic emphasis on present-mindedness and the present time, as it was emphasized by Marcus Aurelius and resurrected by Hadot. This causes problems for any interpretation seeking to link Augustine to Stoicism on topics like mindfulness. Augustine tells us not to live in the moment, but to place our hope in the absolute future of the eschaton, which alone will reveal the proper judgment of these times. For him, there is no real present in which to live. Nowhere is this said more clearly than in a line from the *City of God* (13.11): "the present is sought in the course of times but is not found."[1] There, death was again the problem. It is easy, says Augustine, to say that a living person is not yet dead, just as it is easy to say that a dead person is no longer alive. But to say that someone is dying now, at this very moment, strains our understanding. This is not because death fails to occur, but because dying, like so many processes of transformation, does not take place in an instantaneous present moment (Hannan 2019).

Considered cosmologically, Stoic temporality was also cyclical. All of this has happened before; all of it will happen again. This too is meant to have a therapeutic effect. A focus on the present saves us from anxiety, while the eternal return of the same ensures that everything rests easy in the revolutions of fate's wheel. Augustine could never abide such circularity. It threatened true beatitude, which must be timeless and impossible to lose. Löwith (1949: 163) once wrote that Augustine's argument against the "classical concept of time" is moral in character:

> [The] pagan doctrine is hopeless, for hope and faith are essentially related to the future and a real future cannot exist if past and future times are equal phases within a cyclic recurrence without beginning and end. On the basis of an everlasting revolution of definite cycles, we could expect only a blind rotation of misery and happiness, that is, of deceitful bliss and real misery, but no eternal blessedness—only an endless repetition of the same but nothing new, redemptive, and final.

This moral argument guarantees that Augustinian time will remain linear, though without progressing toward utopia or regressing toward dystopia. Time can be a line without rushing to any value judgment, be it optimistic or pessimistic. In any case, it is no circle.

If time is a line, this need not mean it is made up of points. For Augustine, it means the opposite. For Epicureans like Lucretius, time might bear the structure of a point-like atom; for Stoics like Marcus, it may or may not be atomic in actuality, but it acts like an atom insofar as the human mind is concerned. Contrary to the Epicureans and Stoics, Augustine confronts the possibility that there is no present atom of time whatsoever. Time is *distentio*. Our temporal experience is characterized by belatedness. As a result, we must rely not upon our own present mental state, but upon memory. This is as true of communities as it is of individuals.

The easiest explanation for these differences between Marcus and Augustine is the fact that one is a Stoic and the other is a Christian Neoplatonist. Perhaps it all boils down to a Christian thinker co-opting the Neoplatonic philosophy of time found in Plotinus' third-century *Enneads* (3.7). However, Augustine's account of time is less Plotinian than Aristotelian. Whereas Plotinus develops his analysis alongside a quasi-mythic narrative of the "self-temporalization" of the world-soul (*psyche*) descending from the realm of static mind (*nous*), Augustine deals directly with the hard problems of time-consciousness. Like Aristotle, his interrogation of time and measurement leads him to conclude that there is no real present out there in time itself. The present is not an objective category belonging to what Aristotle calls in the *Physics*

(4.10) the temporal continuum (*sunechēs* or *sunecheia*). The now (*to nun*) is a retrospective construct, which the measuring mind projects onto a continuum in order to divide it up into quantifiable segments. Time, for Aristotle and Augustine, is so linear that it could never really bear within itself the time-atoms of the Stoics or Epicureans. A line, Aristotle reminds us later in the *Physics* (6.1), is not simply a conglomeration of points in a row. To follow the wording of Richard Sorabji (2005: 190), point shall not follow point nor instant follow instant "in such a way that length or time will be composed of these." The timeline is a pure *sunecheia*. If we want to understand time, we must take its nature as a continuum seriously.

With Augustine, we have traveled far from the safe harbor of the present. Stretched apart by the continuum of time, we must cope with the lack of a secure anchorage or a momentary breather. That is why Augustine includes in *Confessions* 11 his threefold description of humankind's psychological reaction to time's distensive force. We cope with the absence of the present by way of memory, awareness, and anticipatory awaiting. None of these faculties, however, can restore the present moment to the heart of temporality. They are stopgap measures aimed at keeping us from coming utterly apart in time. Often, they fail. If not for these psychological consequences of temporality, it might be easy to dismiss the difference between the Augustinian and Stoic accounts of time as ivory-tower hair-splitting. Yet, as Byers also argued, the stakes are real. In her view, there are two reasons for connecting Augustine back to the Stoic theory of agency. The first is reminiscent of mindfulness. Byers (2013: 57) writes approvingly of "the Stoics' advocacy of cognitive therapy, a kind of therapy which, in more recent versions, has had documented success in treating emotional disorders such as depression and anxiety." The second reason makes psychology political. According to Byers (2013: 58), the Stoics predicated their system on "the idea that violent or inappropriate emotions cause catastrophe at the social level." Stoicism is simultaneously a self-help regimen and a social engineering program. While Byers is primarily concerned with fitting Augustine into the psychological and political framework of ancient Stoicism, the pressing concern today is whether or not a similar brand of social engineering lies beneath modern mindfulness.

The Politics of Mindfulness

In terms of thoughtful reflection, the Sunday Review section of the *New York Times* ranks somewhere between a pop-science article on the CNN site and the ethical advice of a scholar like Hadot. The November 26, 2016 edition of the Sunday Review featured an article by Ruth Whippman bearing a memorable title: "Actually, Let's Not Be in the Moment" (Whippman 2016). Whippman tackles the popularity of mindfulness with a more critical edge than CNN's puff piece on Lady Gaga and the Dalai Lama. In so doing, she reveals that mindfulness has become a product to be sold by the very corporations that warp time-consciousness by keeping most folks chained to the punch-clock of industrial time. As a result, the insights of Buddhist and Christian thinkers have been co-opted for ends they never intended. In the *Guardian*, David Forbes made much the same point, arguing that mindfulness is not only a capitalist category, but also an industry in its own right (Forbes 2019). As apps like *Headspace* (https://www. headspace.com) demonstrate, software engineers in California can make millions off of the idea that we should live within the present moment. The now is the most neoliberal phase of time. Augustine might not know what to make of neoliberalism, but he would recognize its characteristic weaknesses, ranging from an over-reliance on our own efforts to an expectation of our just deserts. The presumption that we can bootstrap our way free of time's grasp is consistently undermined by Augustine's engagement with temporality. Our goal should be not to master time from within, but to realize the limits of our own power in the face of temporal *distentio*. Despite the promises of mindfulness products, living in the present remains for Augustine an impossible goal. Marketing such products to the socioeconomic elite might be profitable, but it is also damnable.

Modern moment-worship has political consequences. It is never simply an innocuous matter of how best to reflect in solitude. Meditation in itself has little to stand against it. However, as scholars of Buddhism like Georges Dreyfus (2011: 41–54) have argued, today's self-help literature bears scant resemblance to the contemplative traditions from which it draws. The philosophy of time assumed by corporate mindfulness workshops is seldom similar to that of the ancient Buddhist sages, let alone that of Augustine. It is somewhat more reminiscent of the *Meditations* of Marcus Aurelius. Insofar as these mindfulness products are marketed to powerful people in search of guidance, the philosophy of time they preach cannot be ignored. How we think about time has an effect on the quality of human life in time. If we tell every member of society to live in the moment, we are asking them to adopt a temporal psychology that is not grounded on anything real. Worse, we risk neglecting the role played by social conditions in shaping our everyday experience of time. Here the problem of the present collides with politics. Augustinian *distentio*, which seemed abstract at first, names the concrete conditions under which humankind labors. To pretend that some live in the present more than others is itself a political position. It privileges an exceptional few, such as those who sign up for the right spiritual exercises, at the expense of everybody else. For Augustine, though, time is time. We all inhabit it together in roughly the same way. Being honest with each other about our shared temporal vulnerability will give us a better chance of staying collectively afloat in time than will any attempts to conjure up our own islands of mindful stability.

Augustine comes closest to joining the mindfulness camp in *Confessions* 7 and 9, which recount his contemplative attempts to grasp God's timelessness from within time. The spiritual practices popularized by CNN and Kabat-Zinn find a potential precursor in *Confessions* 7, wherein Augustine attempts in his own mind an isolated ascent to God. This solo flight up to the One is guided by what he learned from the "books of the Platonists," especially Plotinus and Porphyry (CF 7.9.13–7.9.15). Ultimately, his attempt at inner transcendence failed. Augustine's mind was able to climb a few rungs up his conceptual ladder, taking him from the level of sense-perception to that of disembodied ideas, but he could not reach the very top, where the unimaginable divinity resided. The ocean separating temporal from timeless could not be crossed by individual effort. Instead, a bridge had to be built from the other side: the timeless needed to become temporal, so that it could mediate the difference between eternity and time. Augustine needed mediation, not meditation (CF 7.18.24–7.21.27).

This shift from meditation to mediation parallels Augustine's move away from Plotinus' account of temporality in the *Enneads* (3.7). Like Augustine, Plotinus defines time in relation to eternity, which he also takes to be an atemporal state. Unlike Augustine, he frames the time-eternity relationship in terms of his three primary hypostases: the One (*to hen*), the Intellect (*nous*), and the Soul (*psyche*). The inscrutable One lies beyond any shadow of time. To a lesser degree, so does the Intellect, where timeless ideas subsist without change. Only the Soul comes into contact with the temporal world by way of a pre-cosmic Fall. By drifting away from the *nous*, *psyche* temporalized itself. Plotinus, like Mani, is happy to explain the cosmos in mythic terms, though his ode to the fall of *psyche* is less complicated than Manichaean cosmogony.

Furthermore, whereas Mani's myths were meant to stand on their own, Plotinus' narrative lends itself to rational interpretation. It aims to tell us something about how the three primary hypostases relate to one another. This Plotinian triad stands in stark contrast to Augustinian Trinitarianism, especially when we are talking about time. For Augustine, the Father and Son and Holy Spirit are all equally timeless in themselves. The Incarnation of the Son as Jesus of Nazareth is not at all similar to the fall of any world-soul down into matter. *Psyche* is not the bridge between time and eternity. The whole humanity of Christ, body and soul, combines with the divinity of Christ to constitute an entirely distinct hypostasis, which alone is capable of timelessly breaking into the timeline of history.

By the time we get to *Confessions* 9, then, Augustine has found his mediator in Christ, the embodiment of eternity's irruption into temporality. This does not make it easier for Augustine to meditate his way out of time. No longer sitting in isolated reflection, Augustine shares a conversation with his mother Monica as they look down upon a garden in the courtyard of a house in Ostia. The resulting vision at Ostia opens up Augustine's mind to a new way of thinking about the relationship between time and eternity. As he and his mother are discussing the meaning of the phrase "eternal life," which defines the goal of their existence, they are carried away in a reverie that takes them to the limit of their temporal imagination (CF 9.10.24):

When our talk arrived at an end, it seemed like even the greatest delight of the fleshy senses illuminated by the greatest embodied light wouldn't be worth comparing to the pleasure of that eternal life. It wouldn't even be worth remembering. Straightening ourselves up, our feelings aflame for it itself, we walked step by step through all embodied things and even the heavens themselves, through the sun and the moon and the stars that shine their light down on the earth. And here we were climbing even further through your works. Yet we were climbing on the inside. We were climbing by thinking and talking and wondering. When we arrived at our minds, we climbed past those too, so that we could reach out toward a place that is always fertile. That is where you feed Israel the food of truth forever. That is where life is wisdom.[2]

Note that Augustine describes contemplative ascent with the ambiguous language of "reaching," rather than the triumphalist terminology of "comprehending." He and his mother are grasping for something timeless, which does not mean they will actually take hold of it any time soon. What they are looking for cannot be located entirely within their own psychology, since it transcends the mind's timing. They are searching for the same creative wisdom that Augustine identified with truth in his reading of Genesis 1. The next lines in the Ostia passage make the cosmogonic resonances clear (CF 9.10.24):

Through wisdom, everything that has been and will be comes to be. But wisdom itself does not come to be. It is as it was. It is as it will be. Or rather: "have been" and "will be" are not in it. Only "to be" is in wisdom, since it is eternal. And "have been" and "will be" are not eternal. So while we are talking and opening our mouths to drink it all in, we are reaching out to wisdom ever so slightly with every heartbeat. And then we breathed out. We abandoned this early harvest of the Spirit there because it was bound to that place. We then retraced our steps back to our noisy mouths, with their words that begin and end. How are they in any way like your Word, our Lord, which remains in itself without getting old and yet makes all things new?[3]

Augustine sticks doggedly to this vocabulary of reaching, avoiding any claims of secure comprehension. He and his mother approach the boundary-marker between time and eternity, only to be bounced back into the temporal realm of language and community. It is not yet their time. Rather than stepping outside of time's river, Augustine and Monica are brought only to the river's edge. The account of the Ostia vision is shot through with language contrasting time against eternity, not because it tells of successful entry into eternity in the present moment, but because it anticipates, with a lyrical hint of lamentation, eschatological entry into eternity.

For Augustine as for Monica, there is no escape from time now. Their shared vision remains an instructive failure. It brings them back down to earth. Along the way, they learned that contemplation is not an accomplishment of the individual, but a consequence of living in conversation and community with others. The goal in this life is not to escape from the temporal contours of the communities we inhabit, but instead to reckon with the pasts and futures of those communities (as the *City of God* will do). Our ability to focus on the past and future counts for more than present-mindedness. The fundamental illusion is that we think we are bound to the now in the first place. If it turns out that there is no present moment, however, then we have to rethink the way we talk about our temporal experience. The consequences of rethinking time can be therapeutic or sociopolitical, as the Stoics showed. Therapeutically, rethinking time along Augustinian lines suggests healthy skepticism as the best response to modern mindfulness products. Politically, it means we cannot retreat into the now at the expense of what was or will be. Augustine arrives at a new formulation of an old question: How then shall we, as a community, live? Shall we live in the moment or beyond it?

Conclusion

From an Augustinian standpoint, the problems plaguing present-mindedness in antiquity apply just as well to mindfulness in modernity. But is there really a connection between these ancient and modern schools? According to mindfulness advocates like Jon Kabat-Zinn, there is such a connection, though it binds twenty-first-century science back to Buddhism instead of Stoicism. Whereas Hadot preferred to dwell in the Stoic present, Kabat-Zinn appealed to Buddhist philosophy as it developed out of the Abhidharma. According to him, he and the followers of Siddhartha Gautama agree that the secret to life consists in a regimen of present-centered, non-judgmental awareness.

Not all scholars of Buddhism agree with Kabat-Zinn, however. Georges Dreyfus, for example, has argued that what today's psychologists mean by mindfulness is not the same as what ancient thinkers had in mind. Dreyfus (2011: 42) is skeptical of what he calls "a non-elaborative and non-judgmental present-centred awareness." His reason is that classical Buddhist texts, from the writings of Buddhaghosa to the *Questions of King Milinda*, present "mindfulness" not as present-mindedness, but as a mode of temporal engagement characterized by memory.

Even the Sanskrit term translated as "mindfulness" (*smrti*) is derived from a root (*smr*) linked to remembrance and keeping in mind, says Dreyfus (2011: 45). Buddhaghosa once remarked that the function of mindfulness is "not to forget" (Dreyfus 2011: 45). Its aim is to preserve the image of the perceived object over time, not to disregard past data. It is not unlike Augustine's "awareness" (*contuitus*), derived from a root having to do with "guarding" or "watching over" (*tueri*).

Both Augustinian temporality and Buddhaghosa's *smrti* dislocate the present from the center of time. "Mindfulness proper," in Dreyfus' view (2011: 51), becomes "retentive focus." The goal is not to live in the now, but to perceive the temporal world in a way that grants insight (*vipaśyana*) into Buddhist teachings about impermanence, interdependent origination, and the dissolution of the self. The means to this end is not present-mindedness, but retentive memory.

The past matters more than the present. Similar insights led Augustine to emphasize the belatedness afflicting our temporal experience. We think we live in the present, until we try to stop and think about the nature of our experience. Reflection reveals to us the fact that what we take to be present is usually that which has just past. Even some of today's mindfulness advocates concede that we never really free ourselves from the immediate past. Richard Sears (2014: 26), for example, writes the following in his self-help book: "research shows that the thinking brain is at least half a second behind reality. Our senses perceive reality, then thoughts arise. It can be an odd experience to realize that our thinking is not in the present moment, but usually a little bit behind what is going on around us." Any constructive path forward in the conversation between Augustinianism, the Buddhist tradition, and the mindfulness movement should begin with the role played by memory.

The non-evaluative character of mindfulness, meanwhile, could survive the surgical removal of the present from the heart of time. Foregrounding memory goes hand in hand with the idea that we should not leap to conclusions when judging the current state of affairs. Without memory and anticipatory awaiting, awareness of the present situation will not get us far. Given the fact that the future of things can turn out to be quite different from what the present would indicate, a more holistic approach to time-consciousness is needed. Augustine and Buddhaghosa understood this. A myopic focus on the present risks foreclosing future possibilities for individuals and communities alike.

5

The Instant of Indecision

Possibility of Personal Change

Introduction

In *Confessions* 11, Augustine was pulled apart by the distensive force of time. Retrospectively, in the first ten books of the same work, he expressed what it was like to live belatedly in the wake of a dead present. Later, in the *City of God*, he applied that sense of belatedness to the eschatological scope of human history. In each case, the role of memory loomed ever larger as the past threatened to replace the present at the center of temporality. There was, however, at least one conspicuous moment of transformation in Augustine's life story: his conversion, when he seemed to pull himself together in the present instant. Yet his conversion was no smooth process. In rhetoric that should be familiar by now, he writes of being pulled this way and that, thinking he knows what he wants, but not being able to get a firm hold on his own thoughts. The tension mounts as he approaches that unimaginable instant when he will finally decide to follow the God he thought he wanted to follow.

Unfortunately, for Augustine, "the instant of decision is madness." The quotation is attributed to Søren Kierkegaard but repeated more often by Jacques Derrida (1978: 31; 1992: 9).

With the phrase *"l'instant de la décision est une folie,"* Derrida was suggesting the impossibility of a moment when time would freeze and we would have present before us all the information needed to make a truly justifiable decision. As it happens, the river of time runs too fast to freeze; we never do have all the information on hand. Still, decisions are made. Geoffrey Bennington (2011: 103–27) has written an article tracing the tortuous lineage of this citation from Kierkegaard to Derrida. It derives from Kierkegaard's *Philosophical Fragments*, written under the pen name Johannes Climacus. What is at issue there is not the philosophical integrity of the temporal instant, but the possibility of new knowledge. Climacus is arguing against a Socratic model of anamnesis, according to which all knowledge is akin to recollecting something long forgotten. There would then be no radical awakening, no moment when new knowledge is gained where there was none before. Such a result is unacceptable for Climacus, who wants to experience an intellectual breaking point capable of signaling true change. This is the phantom instant of decision he is chasing. Calling this instant "madness" is not, in fact, Kierkegaard's claim or even Climacus'. It is instead a polemical characterization of the Socratic position, which allegedly denies all such instants, decrying them as foolishness (Bennington 2011: 111–14).

Through the historical accidents of language, Kierkegaard's foolishness became Derrida's madness. Both refer to turning-points of one kind or another, and the phrase they both helped popularize remains strangely suited to the scenario of Augustine's conversion. As he approaches his own instant of transformation, Augustine is plagued by a torment not unlike madness. He wants to change his life by reorienting himself toward God, but the power of decision resides in the aspect of time that gives him the most trouble: the present moment. The free choice to convert instantaneously presumes an instant in which to convert. But such an instant is precisely what is lacking. Here again Stoic platitudes ring in our ears. As one of the interlocutors in Epictetus' *Discourses* (1.12; Epictetus 2014: 31) asks with unmistakable incredulity bordering on outrage: "What, is freedom madness, then?" The response arrives straightaway: "Heaven forbid! For freedom and madness are hardly compatible with one another." Augustine was not so sure of this incompatibility of freedom and madness.

Just as relevant as the agony leading up to the mad instant of decision is the turmoil waiting in its aftermath. Augustine's post-conversion life continued to show symptoms of the same afflictions and crises that characterized his earlier years. Augustine explored this ambiguous experience of life after conversion most poignantly in a very late text called *The Gift of Perseverance*. There we read of how true conversion involves the survival of a maddening delay, long after the triumphant climax of *Confessions* 8. The logic of perseverance, as Augustine lays it out for us, is a necessary aspect of the temporality of conversion. Perseverance is, to be blunt, conversion's future.

Searching for Stability

Before we arrive at the dramatic conversion scene, *Confessions* 8 tells us of Augustine's life as a young professional in Milan, where he was making money off his oratorical skills and ascending up the social ladder. Yet, even as he was by all accounts succeeding, he was becoming disgusted with himself and his pointless goals. Having expanded his mind by reading the Platonists in *Confessions* 7, he had also made his break with the Manichaeans complete. He could no longer look past his own secular ambitions by finding hope in their message of salvation in the light.

Despite these tectonic intellectual shifts, it did not feel to Augustine as if much of consequence had changed in his own life. It began to dawn on him that what he was looking for was not more certainty about God or the world, but more stability in God and the world (CF 8.1.1):

> So I no longer wanted to be more certain about you. What I wanted was to be more stable in you. But in my own temporal life everything was wavering. My heart still had to be cleansed of its old, boiling passion.[1]

Temporality remains a problem. Shifting from a Manichaean to a Neoplatonic view of the deity did not pull Augustine out of the river of time. "Everything was wavering": the sentiment applies as much to *Confessions* 4 as to *Confessions* 8. At every stage of life, temporal things crash down on us like waves, while our desires burn us up from within. The result can only be a boiling passion.

No philosophical formulas can fix this condition. Feeling strangely motivated to go and speak to Simplicianus, a revered Christian teacher in Milan, Augustine heard from him the story of Marius Victorinus. Much like Augustine, Victorinus had been convinced by Neoplatonic arguments about the timeless, immaterial nature of true divinity. Yet this did not keep him from his involvements in society, including the observation of polytheistic rites. When Simplicianus pointed out the hypocrisy of this and urged Victorinus to worship within the walls of the church, Victorinus responded acerbically (CF 8.2.4), "So it is walls that make a Christian?"[2] As it turns out, the answer is a qualified yes; the *City of God* clarifies the relevant qualifications. Eventually, Victorinus openly proclaimed his faith, and the community of the faithful rejoiced (CF 8.2.5). A lost soul was redeemed. But this forces Augustine to ask: would it not be happier if that soul were never lost in the first place? It would certainly be stabler. Humankind, however, lives in the space between loss and victory, adversity and prosperity (CF 8.3.6–7). In addition to the arising and passing away of things, there is also an affective arising and passing away of joy and sorrow (CF 8.3.8):

> Everywhere greater joy is preceded by greater troubles. Why is this, Lord? Why is it like this, my God, even though you yourself are eternal joy for yourself, and those who come from you are always rejoicing around you? Why is it that this aspect of things alternates between lack and growth, failures and gains? Or is this their limit? Is this as much as you gave them, when you positioned all kinds of goods and all your just works in their proper places and led them to their proper times, from the heights of heaven to the ends of the earth, from the beginning to the end of the ages, from the angels to the worms, from the first move down to the last?[3]

Just as it is unwise to rely on temporal things that are born to pass away, so is it ill advised to assume that particular situations will last. In *Confessions* 4, Augustine uncovered the limit of things as it pertains to their existence; here, this limit bears also upon the quality of their existence. The order into which we are born is always changing and never lasts. Victorinus' triumphant tale bears within it a chilling lesson about the inconstancy of our unstable desires. Even our desire to hear stories of escape from this wavering world shows how embedded we are in that world.

Such confusions as these put Augustine's conversion on hold. That is why he writes so much about delay and hesitation. He describes his own psyche as a rising up of one will against another. Though he wanted to emulate Victorinus' success story, wanting it was not enough (CF 8.5.10):

> I was held back, not by someone else's iron sword, but by my own iron will... Yet a new will began to be for me, so that I could worship you freely and want to enjoy you, God. You alone are certain pleasure. But this new will was not yet fit for overcoming the old hardness that was already there. And so my two wills—one old, the other new; one fleshly, the other spiritual—were fighting against each other. They were scattering my soul with their discord.[4]

As in *Confessions* 11, Augustine writes here of the violent tearing-apart of his soul. The chains ripping at his flesh are many, from the force of habit to the machinations of Satan. It is his own volition that pains him most, however. Many wills (*voluntates*) arise in opposition to one another within him. As Sarah Byers (2007: 114–17; 2013: 222–3) has shown, the Augustinian will is not a distinct faculty within a pseudo-Platonic psychology. Augustinian wills are more like Stoic dispositions afflicting the soul in its entirety. However, Augustine refuses to combine this Stoic sense of the will with an equally Stoic emphasis on the present moment. Rather than dwelling in the now and gaining clarity about his own goals, Augustine is coming to sense that the question of what he wants has no straightforward answer. When he reflects upon volition, he finds more than he expected. His conversion is not the turning-around of a unitary will that is merely pointed in the wrong direction. Instead, it is more like the turning-together (*con-versio*) of the diversity of wills he is discovering within himself.

Augustine now knew he was running late for his own conversion. He needed a moment of transformation that could gather up his wills and draw them all in the right direction. Yet every time he looked for such a moment, it was not there for him to seize. He likens the experience to trying to wake up and failing. Augustine's was an extreme case, since it was God who was trying to get him out of bed (CF 8.5.12):

> You were saying to me, "Get up! Stop sleeping! Rise from the dead! Christ will illuminate you." But there was no response from me. From all sides, You were showing me that You were telling the truth. But even though I was overcome by the truth, I had no response at all, except for some slow, sleepy words: "In a moment." "Look, I will get up in a moment." "Give me a little bit." But this "moment" had no measure. This "little bit" was getting long.[5]

God is trying to wake Augustine up to a moment of instantaneous transformation. Yet Augustine is not living through any such moment. It is not that he cannot conceive of it at all; he can. But the instant of upheaval never arrives. Now is always just around the corner. It is a *modo* without *modus*, as he puts it. Delay interrupts the instant, giving it the extra duration needed to keep time flowing onward. Augustine is powerless to compact the duration of this delay into a punctual stigma of conversion. He experiences this powerlessness as sleepiness, sluggishness, or, as he suggested elsewhere, belatedness.

Even in *Confessions* 8, then, Augustine is having trouble with time. His search for stability uncovers only instability. His longing for a timely moment or an eye-opening instant is met with deferral. He is late for an auspicious appointment, and it is unclear whether he will arise from his languor soon enough to make it on time. Augustine's book about conversion is thus also about the incessant deferral of change. Few doubt that he did indeed change throughout his life. If, however, we ask the question of when precisely he changed, we find the answer to be not so obvious. This should come as no surprise. Even though Augustine will not explicitly introduce the logic of *distentio* until *Confessions* 11, he is already mobilizing that logic for the description of his own life in the earlier books. In light of *distentio*, his search for a transformative instant would obviously have to result in delay and frustration. In a time without any stable present, any such search is mad.

Volitional *Distentio*

After recounting the Victorinus anecdote, Augustine turns to a scene at the home he and his friend Alypius were sharing in Milan. They are visited by Ponticianus, a fellow African with an impressive military posting. Their visitor strikes up a conversation about Paul, trying to convince Augustine that Paul's epistles merit further attention. Along the way, Ponticianus mentions the Egyptian ascetic Antony. Shocked that Augustine has never heard of Antony, Ponticianus recounts how he first learned of him (CF 8.6.14–15). One day, while posted near Trier, he and some fellow soldiers strolled the gardens near the city wall and stumbled upon a house occupied by "slaves" of God, who owned a copy of Athanasius' *Life of Antony*. Leafing through the text, one of Ponticianus' comrades reflected on the futility of his life compared to Antony. Roman aristocrats, he mused, struggle for a more secure place in the hierarchy, even though the positions near the top are the most precarious. Antony, meanwhile, had all he needed in God. Ponticianus' friend further contrasted the slog of social mobility with the transformative instant of divine favor. "If I want to be a friend of God," he said (CF 8.6.15), "look, I am made one right now."[6] This utterance itself, however, was not the moment of conversion, which came later. As he continued to read, "the flow of his heart changed." The instant of transformation he was looking for had just happened. "I have already broken myself away from our old hopes," he remarked (CF 8.6.15). "I am determined to serve God. It starts now, right here in this place."[7] Ponticianus' friend had just arrived at the idea of instantaneous conversion, and already it was as if it had come to pass.

Augustine was struck by this exemplary conversion, since it was so different from his own experience. As he writes (CF 8.7.17), "I was still deferring taking some time off to investigate wisdom."[8] This deferral was no recent development. It had marked Augustine's life for years. "At the beginning of my youth, still miserable, I had asked you for purity," he recalls (CF 8.7.17). "'Give me purity and self-control,' I had said, 'but not yet!'"[9] This "not yet" applies to the past as he remembers it, as well as to the deferral of change that shapes his life still. The cruelest turn of the screw is that Augustine used to treat deferral as a consequence of insufficient knowledge. He once thought that, if he could learn more about God or the world, he would be able to change. Certainty would breed stability. But this was a lie (CF 8.7.18): "I had thought I was deferring following only you, day after day, in condemned hope for this world, because of the fact that nothing certain appeared to me to guide my way. But the day had come, and I had been stripped bare before myself."[10] The tales of Victorinus and Ponticianus are both exemplary, but examples do little to overcome the deferral of the instant of change.

Once Ponticianus leaves, Augustine sits with Alypius in the garden, overcome by waves of hesitation as his confusion turns into convulsion. His inability to will himself to calm down physiologically hints at an inability to gain stability psychologically. But it is one thing for someone to want to control their body, to stop their teeth from chattering or their knees from trembling, and fail to do so; it is another to want to want something and fail to do so. Augustine wants to be converted to God, and yet he also does not. A kind of madness afflicts the will (CF 8.8.20):

So there I was, doing so many things, even though wanting to do them was not always enough to be able to do them. And I was not doing what would have pleased me much more (the feeling would be incomparable). If I could just want to do that, I would be able to do it as soon as I wanted it, since, as soon as I wanted it, I would want it unconditionally. There, that is where this capacity was. There was the will. There, to want to do it was to have already done it. Still, it was not happening.[11]

At first, Augustine regards our inability to will ourselves to want something as a monstrosity. But it would only be a monstrosity if the will were a unitary thing, incapable of opposing itself. There is, however, a multiplicity of wills. The resulting competition between wills is more malady than monstrosity. It is the inability to draw all those wills together in one shared direction.

Augustine is forced to admit that Mani was right to emphasize volitional multiplicity. For the Manichaeans, opposing wills were evidence of an underlying cosmological dualism. Human life was full of these conflicts because tension was written into the substructure of the universe. Everything referred back to the primordial battle between good and evil, the substance of light and the substance of darkness. Their war played out in the celestial realm and in the microcosm of each bifurcated human being. Even the post-Manichaean Augustine retains an interest in the multiplicity of wills, though he begins to see it as the consequence of an inherited illness called sin. Wills vying against one another can no longer be for Augustine a contest between two substances. One thing, the soul, gets shattered into pieces by its own contrary willing. The same "I" is opposed to itself through a volitional multiplicity (CF 8.10.22):

> When I was weighing whether or not to serve my Lord and God, as I had set out to do so long ago, it was I who wanted to and it was I who did not want to. It was I. I did not fully want to. I did not fully not want to. I was contending with myself. I was being scattered away from myself. This scattering happened to me unwillingly, to be sure. What it was showing me, though, was not the nature of some foreign mind. No, it was showing me the punishment of my own mind. And so I was no longer in control of that mind.[12]

The operation of the mind is conditioned by an involuntary scattering into multiplicity. It is not that Augustine's mind is taken over by another being (that would be too Manichaean), but that his mind loses control of itself to itself. This is the strange psychology of sin, which accommodates a multiplicity of wills going far beyond mere duality.

Augustine next offers a case study. Picture a faithful Manichaean auditor (a lay member of the community, rather than the ascetic elect). The auditor is distracted from religious rites by four distinct diversions, such as the arena, hippodrome, theater, and bordello. The auditor is torn, not between piety and impiety, but between too many impious options. "If all these things occur within one of time's joints," writes Augustine (CF 8.10.24), "if all are equally desired and yet cannot all be done at once, then they tear the soul apart in four wills, all turned away from one another. The soul can be torn into even more wills, as there are so many things to be desired."[13] The Manichaean parallelism between volitional conflict and cosmological dualism begins to look inadequate. Augustine applies this same logic to scenarios featuring multiple good options (CF 8.10.24):

> I might ask [the Manichaeans] whether it is good to delight in a reading of the Apostle or to delight in a sober psalm or to talk about the gospel. And they will respond to each one: "It is good."

Well then, if all of these are equally delightful at the same time, is it not the case that diverted wills stretch apart [*distendunt*] the human heart, as we deliberate about what we should take to be most important? All are indeed good, but they struggle against each other until one is chosen.[14]

Even when faced with nothing but good options, the human heart is "stretched apart" by its "diverted wills." To make sense of the scattering of our souls, we cannot point only to our sinful propensity for evil. Soul-scattering occurs at a more basic level of temporal experience. Volitional *distentio* afflicts all who live their lives under the force of time's *distentio*. Sin is so well suited to time that it becomes difficult to determine whether the overcoming of *distentio* would require the salving of sin, an escape from time, or (more likely) both.

The cure for volitional *distentio* is a *conversio* weighty enough to draw the soul's wills in the same direction. But when could we expect such a great weight to crash down upon us? At this point, Augustine turns back to the problem of the transformative instant. With Alypius sitting there beside him, he finds himself engaged in interior monologue rather than friendly dialogue. Augustine is still trying to will himself to want what he thinks he wants (CF 8.11.25):

Inside myself, I was saying, "Let it happen soon, let it happen soon." With those words, I was already approaching resolution. Already, I was almost doing it, but I was not doing it...I was getting a little bit closer, then a little bit closer still, and then I was starting to touch upon it and take hold of it. Already, I was touching upon it and taking hold of it. Yet I was not there; I was not touching upon it; I was not taking hold of it.[15]

Reaching out for a moment of conversion, Augustine is bounced back, just as he and his mother would be reverberated from the gates of paradise at the climax of their Ostia vision in *Confessions* 9. In the Milanese garden, though, Augustine feels he is drawing closer to a turning-point that could change everything. Yet no such point appears to be on the horizon. He is horrified (CF 8.11.25):

As that point in time when I was going to be something else drew closer and closer, it struck me with more and more horror. But it did not bounce me back again or even turn me away. Rather, it just held me there.[16]

Augustine's conversion should be a *punctum temporis*: a point in time. *Confessions* 11 will teach us how spurious the concept of such a point is. Here, in *Confessions* 8, Augustine expresses what it is like to actually live through the absence of any present *punctum*. As Jean-Luc Marion (2012: 146) observed, Augustine frames his own conversion as an experience in which he both differs from himself and defers the possibility of his own transformation.

The transformative moment Augustine awaits would signal his alteration into something quite different from what he has been in the past. Yet, if conversion is to be punctual, Augustine is already running late, overwhelmed by his multitude of wills. Blaming those wills, he writes (CF 8.11.27): "They were making me late."[17] They are deferring the instant of decision. But they are also part of him. "This controversy in my heart," he continues (CF 8.11.27), "could only be myself turning against myself."[18] Since talking to himself gets him nowhere, Augustine instead quotes Ps. 6:4 as he addresses God about the delay (CF 8.12.28): "And You, Lord? How long? How long will You be angry, Lord? Until the end?" Struck at first by the horror of the disappearance of the present instant, Augustine is now held in suspense. Tomorrow never really becomes today. Nevertheless, like Victorinus, Augustine also gets his happy ending. Leaving Alypius behind, he carries on in a more remote patch of the garden. Even as the voices of his wills pull him apart, he picks out another voice, echoing over from outside the walls. "*Tolle, lege*," it says, sounding like a child: "take it up; pick it up; read." Remembering how Antony's conversion was triggered by obedience to a chance command, Augustine turns at random to a reading from Romans 13 (CF 8.12.29). There he finds moral exhortations suited to his own flaws. He has read Paul's words before, but now they are invested with new significance. "Immediately," he claims (CF 8.12.29), "all the shadows of my hesitation were scattered, as if my heart had been infused with the light of security."[19]

This instant of transformation should be a happy ending, but it is not the end of the story. The *Confessions* continued. The *City of God* and the *Literal Meaning of Genesis* still lay in the future. Augustine's retrospectively triumphalist account of his conversion in *Confessions* 8 must be read alongside these other works, especially if we wish to sort out the complexities of his psychology of temporal experience. The Augustinian impossibility of the instant must be allowed to respond to this account of his apparently instantaneous transformation. To borrow a provocative turn of phrase from Marion (2012: 166), we may need to consider the possibility of Augustine's "non-conversion" in that Milanese garden. No text explores this possibility more rigorously than Augustine's very late *Gift of Perseverance*.

Perseverance and Belatedness

Near the end of his life, Augustine received some concerning letters from monks at Massilia in Southern Gaul. These monks had long thought themselves to be in line with the Bishop of Hippo. But they had heard some unsettling news about Augustine's teachings on grace (Ogliari 2003; Casiday 2005). Around this time, Augustine had been clarifying his position on divine initiative in opposition to the ascetic life-coach Pelagius, who considered grace to be the help God grants Christians as they themselves strive for moral excellence. As the monks learned, Augustine argued against the Pelagians that even the first steps of faith, including conversion, were to be attributed to the agency of God, not humankind. The same could be said of the last steps of faith, taken only when we are at death's door. If this is the case, then the idea of spiritual progress (along the monastic path, for example) might be called into question.

Augustine argues most ardently in defense of grace in his treatise *Predestination of the Saints* and its sequel, *Gift of Perseverance*. The former emphasizes the divine agency lying behind the beginning of faith, while the latter considers the same agency as it stokes the fires of faith throughout the rest of a believer's life. Augustine's attribution of the *initium fidei* to God should not surprise us as it did the monks, since only the divine could overcome Augustine's volitional *distentio*. "You converted me," he once confided to God (CF 8.12.30). The *Gift of Perseverance* is more surprising. There, in what is ostensibly a theological reinterpretation of the meaning of the Lord's Prayer, Augustine brings grace to bear not just upon particular events, but upon the entire duration of a human life. True conversion calls for perseverance until the end of time.

The *Gift* begins by clarifying what perseverance is, especially in light of Augustine's growing sense that *distentio* afflicts even those who have been converted and baptized. "Conversion," as Marion (2012: 145–6) observed, "does not resolve everything." Augustine explicitly links his line of thinking here back to his earlier text *De Quaestionibus ad Simplicianum*, in which he first realized that Paul's account of inner struggle applies to Christian and non-Christian alike (DP 20.53, 21.55). The succinctness of the opening passage of the *Gift* belies the challenging conclusions to be drawn from it (DP 1.1):

We assert that the perseverance by which we persevere in Christ until the end is a gift from God. I am talking about the ending of this life. In this life, there is nothing but the risk of falling, and so it is never certain whether someone has received this gift for as long as that person leads their life. If they fall before they die, it is said that they did not persevere. Nothing could be truer.[20]

It is peculiar to perseverance that it can only belong to those who are no longer there to have it. If some people attend church regularly, for example, and later fall away, they do not truly persevere. They appeared to persevere for a while, but that counts for nothing. The point of perseverance is that it lasts until the end. From the perspective of temporal experience, perseverance is a future gift. "The sins we are asking to be forgiven are past," writes Augustine (DP 5.8). "The perseverance that makes us saved forever, meanwhile, is necessary not for the part of our lifetime that has already happened, but for the time that remains until the end."[21] It would be unwise to ascribe perseverance to anyone still living. It is a special gift, recognizable only in the dead (DP 5.10):

If it is given, someone has persevered until the end. If someone has not persevered until the end, then it was not given ... So let no one say that any perseverance until the end has been given unless the end has come and someone, to whom it has been given, has been found to have persevered to the end.[22]

Such a gift can never be lost, since whoever had it has already ceased to exist by the time we can hazard a judgment as to whether they received it or not. Despite its illegibility, perseverance remains the most important gift. Many people go through the motions of conversion, be they fits of sorrow in a garden or solemn vows in a basilica. But they can always fall away and lose everything. As a result, says Augustine (DP 24.66), "those who do not have this gift have nothing, no matter what else they might have."[23] Appearances of conversion are provisional, since the struggle of perseverance awaits. Judgments about salvation can only be made after the fact.

Retrospective judgments about perseverance take place in and through communities like the monastery at Massilia or the congregation in Hippo. And yet, in a world where perseverance is illegible before death, it becomes difficult to determine who makes up the true community. Some of those who appear to be within the walls will receive the gift of persevering until the end; others will not. It is not the case that there are two natural kinds of humans: persevering ones and non-persevering ones (DP 8.19). That rings too Manichaean. For Augustine, everyone is made of the same stuff, and no one deserves any special favors from God (DP 9.21). The distinction between those who persevere and those who do not is simply a consequence of the divine agency Augustine calls grace (DP 7.15). Human spontaneity does not find itself at the beginning of things. Our agency, like our confessions, is a response. When we try to judge who is on the inside and who is on the outside at any given moment, we are responding to a situation not of our own making. Imagining that every member of a community of faith is already saved is a dangerously proud, stunningly premature enterprise. Quoting 1 Cor. 10:12, Augustine writes (DP 8.19):

It seems to most people that every faithful person who appears to be good ought to receive perseverance until the end. But God has judged it better to mix some who will not persevere in with a certain number of God's saints, so that those who are not free from anxiety in the temptation of this life can never be free from anxiety in this life. Many of us should be discouraged from our dangerously premature celebration by what the Apostle had to say about this: "So those who seem to be standing should see that they do not fall."[24]

Pretence to stability does more harm than good. The community of converts remains a multitude of unsteady souls, caught up in time, ready at any moment to topple. The walls that make a Christian are not so steady that they never crumble. Baptism, too, is unsettled by perseverance. "Even among those who are reborn," says Augustine (DP 13.32), "there are some who persevere and get to the end, while others are held firm up to a certain point and then fall away."[25] Conversion now seems like a less dramatic breaking-point. Augustine's apparent decision to follow God is nothing compared to God's timeless decision about who will persevere until the end. Augustine's own status with regard to the latter decision must remain unclear, at least until his own death. Still, it is that divine decision, not his gesticulations in the garden, that determines the outcome. Judgment about the status of Augustine's salvation is deferred until the end, at which point he will not be the one to make it (CF 13.33).

This might seem a grim situation. The outcome of our lives does not depend on daily progress, as if there were a salvation app on our smartphones tracking our ascent to salvation. The decisions we make that seem so momentous turn out to be consequences of a divine decision made outside of time. The priority of God's decision cannot be overcome, since it is not temporal priority but the priority of a creator over the created. It is reminiscent of the cosmologically causal priority Augustine discussed in his *Literal Meaning of Genesis*, which likewise makes no claims about temporal before and after. The intransigence of our wills and the illegible boundaries of our communities are symptoms of our inability to unseat God or lift ourselves out of determined receptivity and into the divine position of determining spontaneity. Our inability and ignorance are, however, the seeds of hope.

Later in the *Gift*, Augustine shares an anecdote about a monk in Hippo. This monk had not been living up to the standards of his vocation and was called to account for it. In response, he took refuge in what Augustine finds to be a cheap appeal to divine foreknowledge (DP 15.38):

There was a certain someone in our own monastery. His brothers were trying to correct him, seeing that he was doing what should not be done and was not doing what should be done. He responded, "Whatever I may be like now, in the future I will be as God knew in advance I was going to be." What he said was true, of course, but it did not help him advance in goodness. Rather, he advanced so far in evil that he abandoned the community of the monastery and became a dog, turning back to his own vomit. Nevertheless, it is still uncertain what he will be like in the future.[26]

In the wake of every conversion lies the perverse threat of reversion. Despite this monk's arrogance, Augustine uses him to caution against ruling out those who look like they are on the outside. Even in the case of an intransigent monk, it is impossible to foresee where he will end up. The bounds set on our ability to gauge people's lives as they live them signal openness to a future that we humbly acknowledge to be unknowable for us. As John Cavadini (2007: 123–4) observed, Augustine's account of the self in time aims at resisting "a premature foreclosure of identity and yielding to a process that will be complete only eschatologically, and only as a gift partly received and mostly hoped for, and not in the first place as an accomplishment."

In the end, the *Gift* informs us, the distinction between those who will persevere and those who will not can only be recognized in retrospect (DP 22.58). We can never declare our own conversions to have been successful or not, since we fail to encounter an instantaneous moment of transformation that would render our temporal experience more stable. Nor can we securely police the borders of our faith communities, since the proper sorting-out of true converts from false must wait until time itself has reached its limit. But that is always too late for present purposes, when we usually seek to include ourselves and exclude others. Augustine's own break with the past is not as dramatic as he represented it in *Confessions* 8. His wills are still many. He remains in the grip of *distentio*, both volitional and temporal. The question is no longer how much he might improve after conversion, but whether he will be able to hold on in this river of time.

In the *Gift*, Augustine is not looking ahead to victory. There is not much to see up ahead. Instead, he looks backward: to the dead, to those who did not persevere, and to his own conversion. Perseverance deals with the future, but the future cannot be seen. Its invisibility is inviolable, because it safeguards the sovereignty of God's timeless decision and the open-endedness of life in time. Perseverance is the best orientation toward the future for those born looking backward. "Hang on, persevere, tolerate, bear the delay, and you have taken up your cross": this is the advice Augustine gives in one of his sermons (1992: 34). Whether we persevere or not is in the hands of the one who died on the cross. Perhaps for Adam it had been otherwise, but things are not what they used to be. As Augustine explains (DP 7.13): "After the fall of humankind, people can only approach God if God wants them to belong to God's Grace, and people cannot pull away from God unless God does not want them to belong to God's Grace."[27] Augustine quotes Ps. 84:7 to drive his point home (DP 7.13):

Nothing happens except what God makes happen or permits to happen. And so God is able to bend wills from evil to good, turning back [*convertere*] those who are about to fall and putting them on a path that pleases God. "God, you will convert us and bring us to life"; this was not said in vain.[28]

No one, according to Augustine, is strong enough to stabilize themselves in time. No one can will themselves to stand. Only a God could do that (DP 8.19). Rather than thinking we are standing firm or presuming we have converted, we should be afraid that maybe we have not yet converted at all.

But where does all this wavering between standing and falling play out? Augustine provides an answer (DP 8.19): "People stand or fall in their own thoughts."[29] When he begins to talk about thinking, Augustine moves from Paul to a more proximate influence: Ambrose of Milan. It was Ambrose (DP 8.19) who had been "bold enough to say: 'Our hearts and our thoughts are not in our power.' Everyone who is humbly and truthfully pious feels this to be so very true."[30] Cognitive alienation accompanies the illegibility of our lives. Both the *Gift* and *Confessions* 10 agree that we are alienated from our thoughts because we arrive at them belatedly. Our thoughts are not subject to our spontaneity. They happen; we live through them. Augustine quotes from Ambrose's sermon on fleeing the *saeculum*:

Our hearts and our thoughts are not in our power. Thoughts flood our souls unexpectedly and deluge our minds. They drag in something that you did not want to think about. They call you back to worldly things. They insert mundane things. They bring in things that please you and weave in things that entice you. At the very time that we are trying to elevate our minds, we are usually invaded by empty thoughts and thrown down to the earth.[31]

Thoughts rush in, says Ambrose, and we react. This is temporal belatedness framed in cognitive terms. Receptivity is written into our minds, since even thinking derives from some prior, alien spontaneity. Ambrose's homiletic insight resonates with Augustine's comments on volition (in *Confessions* 8), memory (in *Confessions* 10), and time (in *Confessions* 11). All speak of the temporal alienation experienced by the human mind, insofar as it lacks a stable moment in which to be present to itself. This absent present is the blind spot in thinking, the foreign origin of our own thoughts, and (more happily) the opening for grace. We arrive late to the scene of our own thoughts, but in so doing we see that they were already set in motion without our initiative. This need not mean we feel God forcing us to want or think this or that. Rather, we find that we want or think this or that, while also finding that we did not choose to want or think this or that. Our wills and thoughts were given to us as a given for us. The pious thing to do is to attribute that which is given to the one who would have been there in the beginning to give all this: an absolutely primordial creator.

To phrase it concisely alongside Ambrose and Augustine (DP 19.49): "the human will is prepared by God."[32] Human willing operates in terms of what it is given to want. If someone wants to love God, it is because they have been given the will to do so. If they do not, the gift was lacking. In either case, it is what is given or not that is decisive. This is what is not in our power. Even for supposed enemies of the faith, it might turn out that what will be given for them in the future is not what is given for them today. "They do not want it," says Augustine (DP 22.60), "but God makes them want it."[33] Making is giving: it is grace in action. Even the will to ask God for grace and the thought of praying to God for grace are given through grace. No human spontaneity can insert itself back before the divine (DP 23.64):

> This is where we understand that our crying out to God spiritually and with a truthful heart is also a gift from God. Those who think that our asking, our seeking, our knocking comes from us

and is not given to us should pay attention to how mistaken they are. They say that this is why our merit comes before grace, so that grace follows afterward. When we ask for it, we receive it. When we seek, we find. When we knock, it is opened. They do not want to understand that even our praying, our asking, our seeking, our knocking comes from the divine allotment.[34]

Our relationship with grace is retroactive. We ask for what has already been given or not given. We seek what has already come to us or not. We knock on a door that is either already open or never will be. All of our willing and thinking takes place in this context of retrospective receptivity to what came before.

As Augustine tells it, we are wavering between the absolute past of an unimaginable decision and the absolute future of the very end. The time between these two atemporal limit-points is not characterized by stable moments, transformative turning-points, or decisive instants. Deferral, delay, and suspense await us. Alienated from the origin of our thoughts, we come upon them *in medias res*. This lends an indelible hint of belatedness to our experience both of ourselves and of our communities. Grace gives our thoughts a head start on us. We can never catch up, no matter how hard we try. The proper response is not to try harder, deluded by pride into thinking we might gain full control of ourselves. Augustine recommends the less triumphant stance of humble perseverance. Far from catching up to our lives, our best hope is to hold on for dear life. That is what perseverance looks like: living out a distended existence, always a step behind your own mind, ever mindful that things could fall away at any time. Acknowledging belatedness, with its lack of spontaneity and primacy, allows us to spot the opening for grace, which remains no guarantee. "Tremble as you celebrate God, since no one can be sure about eternal life," advised Augustine (DP 22.62), citing Ps. 2:11 and Job 7:1, "until their life, which is a trial on the earth, has come to completion."[35]

Conclusion

Augustine's *Gift of Perseverance* is not silent about his conversion in the Milanese garden. He returns to the scene in order to remind his readers that, even decades before, he wrote the primacy of divine

agency into his own transformation. Recalling his motto from
Confessions 8, he writes (DP 20.53): "Give what you command
and command what you will." The conversion scene merely puts
these words to work (DP 20.53):

> In those same books [of the *Confessions*], I told the story of my
> conversion. As God was converting me to the faith, I was laying
> waste with a furious but pitiful verbosity. Do you not remember
> how I told the story that way, so I could show that I had been
> given up to the faithful tears my mother cried every day over
> my perishing? There, I absolutely preached that God converts
> human wills to faith by His grace.[36]

Next he adds (DP 20.53): "There, too, I asked God about ongoing
perseverance."[37] The triumphant ending of *Confessions* 8 is forced
to make room for perseverance, which better suits Augustine's sense
of belatedness and *distentio*. His account of conversion and his
argument about perseverance can thus be read together, though not
without difficulty. That is why works like the *Gift* had to be written
in the first place. An overly idealistic view of post-conversion life
had distorted the worldviews of Pelagius and (to a lesser degree)
the monks of Massilia. Augustine's work on perseverance aims to
correct their optimistic overreach. He does so not by innovating
from scratch, but by returning to the logic of his earlier arguments
about time and agency in the *Confessions*. At every turn, he is at
pains to show how the duration of conversion is drawn out until
the end, staying illegible for those who still live.

Conversion is less about the mad instant of decision than it is
about the inscrutable hiddenness of a timeless determination. The
instant of decision is *folie*, not as clinical madness, but as the folly
of presumption. Taking the span of a human life into account, the
turning-point of conversion is far from the determining factor. At
most, it is a retroactively posited point, itself a response to the prior
spontaneity conditioning our experience. Our access to primordial
spontaneity, however, remains strictly limited. Augustine's life
story was written out in advance, but in a script he could never
read. Perseverance expresses this illegibility by postponing the
interpretation of someone's life until they are no longer living it.
As the rhetoric of belatedness in *Confessions* 4 and *distentio* in
Confessions 11 suggests, Augustine holds that all measurement in

time is retrospective. With his work on perseverance, Augustine is telling us that this goes for how a person's life measures up, just as much as it does for our attempts to take the measure of all human history, as the *City of God* made clear. Building on the work of James Wetzel (1992), Susannah Ticciati (2010: 417) concisely summarized Augustine's position as follows: "grace has been at work all along, but can only be seen to have been so in retrospect."

6

The Time Is Not Now

Activism Despite Quietism

Introduction

The Sermon on the Mount, as recounted in the Gospel of Matthew, contains some potentially contradictory statements about time. In Mt. 6:34, Jesus warns against getting too anxious about tomorrow. Advice like this might remind us of those who define mindfulness as present-mindedness. But here again the words used include within themselves the seeds of their own critique. As Dreyfus showed us, Sanskrit *smrti* has more to do with retentive memory than living in the now. Matthew 6 offers a similar case of temporal slippage. The term rendered as anxiety or care (*merimna*) has roots in the Greek vocabulary of memory (from *mnēmē* to *anamnēsis*). It is as though we are being advised to avoid anxiety by refusing to remember the future. The word taken as tomorrow (*aurion*) is relatively uncontroversial, though it becomes more interesting once we set it alongside a line of the Lord's Prayer in Mt. 6:11: "Give us today (*sēmeron*) our daily (*epiousion*) bread." This use of *epiousion* has occasioned much dispute, though most agree that "daily" is not the best translation. Two more probable options are "super-natural" (above that which is: *epi-ousia*) and "tomorrow's" (in the sense of the day that is almost upon (*epi-*) us). In the latter case, Mt. 6:11 would be imploring us to pray: "Give us today tomorrow's bread."

And so the Lord's Prayer also leaves us with food for thought concerning our relationship to time. Perhaps this is why Augustine structured his text on perseverance as a theologically imaginative rereading of the words of that prayer. Augustine, whose Greek was not perfect, has little to say about the dailiness of his bread in the *Gift*; he is content to take it in the "everyday" sense of his Old Latin edition's *quotidianum*. Still, invoking no less an authority than Cyprian of Carthage, he notes that even this passage of the paternoster pertains to perseverance (DP 7.4).

While Augustine's Latin phrasing would permit him to locate this "bread" in the present, he instead connects it straightaway to the future of temporal experience, determined as it is by perseverance as a gift. To receive each day our daily bread does not necessarily mean we must live in the present with no thought for the morrow. It could just as well, for the Greeks and even for the Latinized African Augustine, mean receiving the future.

Augustine's reception of the New Testament in general left him with a series of temporal ambiguities. As Matthew 6 suggests, the question is not just: "what is time?" We also have to ask: "what time is it?" Do Christians live in an already-redeemed present age? Or must they let their anxiety pull them ahead into tomorrow? The ambiguity only deepens if we turn from Matthew's Gospel to Paul's letters. There we find the Pauline rhetoric of the *kairos*, a special kind of messianic time. Like Matthew, however, Paul can be read in many ways. Some saw him as an apocalyptic herald, ushering in an imminent end; others saw him as creating communities meant to last until a more eschatologically distant future. These two readings of Paul could give rise to different ways of mobilizing the philosophy of time for the sake of politics, theology, and political theology.

Nowhere is the modern appeal of Paul's *kairos* more evident than in the works of Giorgio Agamben. Writing in the wake of mid-twentieth-century political unrest, Agamben found in Paul the promise of a revived *kairos*. The new messianic temporality would not necessarily remain Christian, but it would become revolutionary. Some kind of event, construed as a radically transformative moment, would be needed if the entire historical trajectory of humankind were to be changed for the better. For Agamben, the time must, in some sense, be now. But what time was it for Augustine? Was it today or is it tomorrow?

Augustine would be unlikely to place transformative social change in the present, given its spurious constitution. But does this make Augustine a political quietist? The suspicion has occurred to many of his readers (Dassmann 1996; Kaufman 2003; Lee 2016). Few have framed their accusations as harshly as Virginia Burrus. Augustine's "strategies of displacement and deferral" attest to his "mistrust of the flesh of history," writes Burrus (1999: 193), adding that his failures are not "accidental but inherent to the structure of his apocalypticism." By refusing to read the so-called signs of the times in expectation of an imminent end, Augustine is foreclosing the possibility of historical transformation. Resigning himself to an inherently conservative quietism, he becomes an anti-prophet. The risk suggested by Burrus is a real one, though this does not mean that such accusations of quietism amount to the last word on Augustine's temporal politics. We are still permitted to ask: are these accusations fair? Does Augustine's muted apocalypticism make political transformation (or even revolution) unthinkable on the grounds of Augustinian temporality? To find out, we will have to approach Augustine anew one last time by way of Paul, Agamben, and two unexpected but unarguably relevant interlocutors: Malcolm X and Martin Luther King, Jr.

The Clock and the River

Agamben is hard to categorize as a thinker. He often works with historical sources, but with an eye to their ongoing philosophical and political applications. Walter Benjamin is his kindred idiosyncratic spirit, but Agamben also loves to cite ancient and medieval Christian literature as he goes about diagnosing modern maladies, ranging from biopolitical surveillance to the proliferation of concentration camps. While he is not alone among contemporary philosophers in his return to Christian sources, he should be singled out for the care shown in his approach to Christianity. Agamben's engagement with Paul, for example, convincingly connects the Apostle's messianism to the problem of the present in our own era. His more recent publications have continued to explore the interconnectedness between how we think of time and how we shape our political communities. Keeping to our spirit of temporal dislocation, then, we should begin with the later Agamben before moving back to the earlier.

The Highest Poverty, the first part of the fourth stage of Agamben's *Homo Sacer* project, argues that medieval cenobitic monasticism helps us think our way toward what he calls form-of-life, in which our lives become virtually indistinguishable from the rule by which we live. Central to this model is the regulation of time via the hours of the offices. A series of prayers and activities punctuated the monk's day, thereby structuring temporal experience in a way that was not evident in nature. This "chronometric scansion of human time," as Agamben (2013: 18–19) named it, is both the "monastic precedent" for the iron cage of industrialized temporality and the key to unlocking that cage. The Weberian notes are hard to miss. Instead of living under the law of the industrial punch-clock, the cenobites transformed themselves into timepieces of their own lives. Agamben (2013: 20) refers to the eleventh-century Benedictine Peter Damian, who once remarked that the goal of the monk is to become "a certain sort of clock" (*quoddam Horologium*).

For the most part, Agamben uses as his model the spiritual Franciscans, since they raised pertinent questions of utility, ownership, and community in the late thirteenth and early fourteenth centuries. He adds, however, that he could just as well have relied upon the sixteenth-century humanist Rabelais' satirical description of Thélème, a fictional monastery associated with a grotesque giant named Gargantua. In his *Vie très horrifique du grand Gargantua*, Rabelais tells us how the hours and offices of Thélème inverted the temporal logic of the usual monastery. As Agamben (2013: 5) describes them:

> [B]ecause in the monasteries of this world everything is compassed, limited, and regulated by hours, it was decreed that there should never be any clock or sundial whatsoever, but all works would be dispensed according to occasions and opportunities; for, Gargantua used to say, the greatest waste of time he knew of was to count the hours—what good comes of that? And the greatest folly in the world was to govern oneself by the ring of a bell and not at the dictation of good sense and understanding.

Mocking temporal measurement, Gargantua undermines humankind's attempts to tame time. At Thélème, the right time to do something is whenever one feels like it. There is no need to wait for an auspicious moment, let alone something so quotidian as the ringing of a church bell. For monks like Damian, however, the ringing of the bell is of utmost importance. It must never be too early or too late. The punctuality of the hours has to be observed. According to Agamben (2013: 21), this "hourly scansion of existence" seeped down into twenty-first-century time-consciousness. Today, continues Agamben (2013: 24), we are preconditioned to "articulate our existence according to times and hours and to consider even our interior life as a linear and homogeneous course of time." He adds that this monastic conditioning of time-consciousness has had far more of an effect upon the lives of individuals and communities than Stoicism's therapeutic temporality ever could. As proof, we need only consider how natural it feels for us to time our activities, be they undertaken as labor or as leisure. The poetry of monastic time has devolved into the crude clockworks of industry and its corollary: allotted vacation time.

Alongside Damian and Rabelais, Agamben ranges a series of cenobitic authors, from Basil the Great to Bonaventure, the hero of the spiritual Franciscans. At times, he alludes to Augustine, who may have written the Rule that bears his name. But while Augustine is known for having something to say about time, it is not clear that Augustinian temporality maps onto the horological vision of Christian time Agamben is developing. When Augustine interrogates time, what he uncovers is not the rigor of punctuality, but the elusiveness of the present, which leads us to run late in our attempts to put in the hours (to the detriment of industry) or be present in this life (to the detriment of popular mindfulness). Agamben's project might then be subject to reappraisal in light of Augustinian temporality. To test this hypothesis out, we will have to turn away from *The Highest Poverty* and look to older works like *Infancy and History* or *The Time That Remains*, where Agamben frames the present in terms of the messianic now he found in Paul's letters. Agamben's aim is to revivify this messianic present for the sake of social transformation. Augustine's critique of time, meanwhile, renders the present inoperable, which nevertheless does not render social transformation impossible.

Paul, for his part, may not have foreseen the legions of philosophers who would eventually mine his every word for usable conceptual content. *Kairos*, a Pauline term for time that cannot be reduced to *chronos* (time *simpliciter*), has proven especially irresistible in this regard. But Paul sought neither to define time nor to pontificate on its measurement. He was more interested in the shortening lifespan of the world as we know it. Time, for Paul, was bounded by a definite end: the passing away of the form of this world. Everything he had to say about the past, present, and future was conditioned in advance by this urgency and finality.

Within this framework, *kairos* can bear a range of meanings: season, occasion, opportunity, event, and so on. Appropriately, Paul's epistles treat temporality in relation to world-shaping events. Unlike *chronos*, the temporality of *kairos* is not a value-neutral flux. It names the appropriate time, the auspicious time, or the right time. It is the time for something to be done. As a result, it carries a heavier burden than does *chronos*. This is not to say that there is just one *kairos*-event. According to Paul, multiple *kairoi* can take place in the past, present, and future.

The obvious exemplar of a past *kairos* is the moment of Christ's death. In Rom. 5:6, Paul writes that "at just the right time [*kata kairon*], when we were still powerless, Christ died for the ungodly." The timing of this death was not accidental. It occurred while humankind was weak and lost. Paul uses the notion of the *kairos* to teach his readers that they did nothing to earn the sacrifice of Christ. It was given freely. Related to this use of *kairos* is the Pauline phrase "the fullness of time." There is a fullness (*plērōma*) to the auspicious time at which the events of salvation history occur. Empty time (*chronos*) gets filled up with significance at these key junctures. In Gal. 4:1-5, Paul adds that even before the crucifixion, the incarnation of Christ signaled the arrival of temporal fullness. Similar sentiments can be found in the deutero-Pauline epistles (Eph. 1:9-10). Both the birth and death of Christ might then count as past *kairoi*, although it is simpler to just name the entire Christ-event a *kairos*. The fullness of time is capable of expanding to include the entire stretch of a human life within one kairological snapshot.

At the end of Paul's temporal spectrum resides the eschaton. This is the absolute future: a horizon beyond which normal ways of talking about time no longer make sense. It is the mirror image of Lemaître's timeless moment of creation, before which time likewise means nothing. There *chronos* reaches its limit, but *kairos* survives. In 1 Cor. 4:5 (one of Augustine's favorite passages), Paul invokes this eschatological *kairos* to drive home his ethical teachings about humility in the face of others' perceived moral failings. No one, said Paul, should feel entitled to rush to judgment against another. Now was not the time for that. Severe judgment could only be deferred to a time beyond time or a *kairos* beyond *chronos*. "Judge nothing before the appointed time [*pro kairou*]," was his advice, "wait until the Lord comes. He will bring to light what is hidden in darkness and will expose the motives of the heart. At that time, each will receive their praise from God." The *kairos* of judgment is postponed until the last times. In 1 Thess. 5:1-2, however, Paul denies having particular knowledge of apocalyptic dates. He writes to the Thessalonians about neither empty times (*chronoi*) nor meaningful times (*kairoi*). The fact that God arrives like a thief in the night suggests we should not waste our time clock-watching. 2 Thess. 2:6-7 is more ominous, hinting ahead to the *kairos* at which the Lawless One will be revealed to have been retroactively at work throughout humankind's past.

Between the Christ-event and final judgment lies a third *kairos*, which Paul takes to be in effect as he writes his letters. The incarnation, crucifixion, and resurrection had initiated a season of opportunity for those who believed in them as world-altering events. According to Rom. 11:5, these believers constitute a messianic community in this time that is now (*ho nun kairos*). 2 Cor. 6:12 aims to reassure such a community that they are living in the "time (*kairos*) of God's favour" as foretold by Isa. 49:8. Yet Paul continues to warn against getting comfortable, since this remains a time of urgency. 1 Cor. 7:29-31 is one of his more urgent passages:

What I mean, brothers and sisters, is that the time is short (*ho kairos sunestalmenos estin*). From now on those who have wives should live as if they do not; those who mourn, as if they did not; those who are happy, as if they were not; those who buy something, as if it were not theirs to keep; those who use the things of the world, as if not engrossed in them. For this world in its present form is passing away.

With time's shortness and the world's passing, Paul frames this present *kairos* of opportunity in relation to the future's eschatological *kairos*, as well as to the past *kairos* of the messiah's lifetime. Gal. 6:7-10 sets one *kairos* alongside the other, suggesting a moral calculus: if we do good work in this opportune season, we will reap the harvest at the proper time, which has for that very reason not yet arrived. It would be unwise to plant the seed and dig it back up on the very same day. For the Apostle, it is incumbent upon all to understand the *kairos*. But understanding the *kairos* requires understanding the many *kairoi* which proliferate once we stop to reflect on the hidden architecture of salvation history.

The Pauline community of believers is therefore bound together in an age of transformation, held in tension and stretched apart between the first and second advents of their messiah. This imagery of stretching can also be found in Philippians, where Paul advises believers against worrying about the practices of their brethren who observed ritual dictates found in the Hebrew Bible. He himself, he writes, has rejected these traditions. The world itself, in its passing away, has become like refuse in his eyes. That is the mindset his fellow believers must adopt. Since this makes Paul sound overly confident, he is quick (in Phil. 3:12-14) to assert in humility that ascetic heights remain an ideal target:

> Not that I have already obtained all this, or have already arrived at my goal, but I press on to take hold of that for which Christ Jesus took hold of me. Brothers and sisters, I do not consider myself yet to have taken hold of it. But one thing I do: Forgetting what is behind and straining out toward what is ahead, I press on toward the goal to win the prize for which God has called me heavenward in Christ Jesus.

What Paul stretches out toward is the eschaton, when it will finally be time to end time. And yet, despite what Paul says here about "forgetting," the past *kairos* of the messiah's lifetime cannot be abandoned. The Augustinian question becomes: what is it like to live in between these two Pauline limit-points? The *saeculum* stretches out between the Christ-event and the eschaton.

Augustine, however, is not as sanguine about the present time as Paul might have been. The *saeculum* is barren ground, not a season of opportunity. The specious present of psychological or historical reflection has been built on shifting sands. At the heart of temporal experience, we find structural vulnerability. We find a wound. The only salve for this wound is salvation. The unimaginable heat of divine love awaits at time's end. Some it cauterizes; others it burns. In relation to eternity, time can only be pain (Wyschogrod 1990).

If God is fire, time is water. In the year 415 CE, during Eastertide, Augustine delivered a series of sermons now known as the *Homilies on 1 John.* He delivered these homilies in response to the Donatist schism between Christian communities which threatened to rend the social fabric of North Africa. Factionalism had long plagued cities like Augustine's Hippo, dating back to sporadic persecutions under the Emperor Decius in the middle of the third century and Diocletian at the beginning of the fourth. The result was a split between Augustine's universalists, who sought communion with the rest of the Mediterranean world, and localist groups, who wished to preserve a true remnant of the faithful. These pious locals rejected the legitimacy of sacraments performed by clerics they deemed *traditores* or ordained by *traditores*. To be a *traditor* meant being a traitor: someone who turned the scriptures over to the authorities for destruction. This was a grave crime for both Augustine and his enemies. The difference was that, for Augustine, the joint powers of forgiveness and sacramentality overcame even this transgression. His opponents, who came to be known as the Donatists, disagreed. By 411 CE, Augustine and his allies had begun to tip the scales in their own favor with the Council of Carthage. The *Homilies on 1 John* were composed in the wake of this seminal but not final victory.

But what does the Donatist controversy have to do with the problem of temporality? How do we get from Augustine's polemics to his philosophy of time? As it turns out, all three of Augustine's premier polemical targets played a role in sharpening his appreciation for our struggles in time. Manichaean cosmogony provided the backdrop for his cosmological exploration of time's beginning and end. Pelagius' fanaticism of free choice, meanwhile, flummoxed the aged Augustine so much that he perhaps wrote more treatises than necessary against the untrammeled sovereignty of the instant of decision. The Donatist controversy, too, led Augustine to reconsider the ultimate value of whatever entices us in time, even in the arenas of politics and ecclesiology. The goal of social mastery evaporates in view of eternity.

Our higher goal is to find safer shores, not to get lost in the dream of time's river running dry. Unfortunately, we cannot make the shores come to us. The timeless must break through into time. This is where the messiah comes in; this is where Christ mediates between timeless and temporal. But if time is a river, then what is Christ? According to Augustine (1955b: 275; HJ 2.10), Christ is a tree:

Make your choice: either to love things temporal and pass away with time's passing, or not to love the world, and to live forever with God. The river of time sweeps us on; but there, like a tree growing by the river, is our Lord Jesus Christ. He took flesh, died, rose again, ascended into heaven. He willed to plant himself as it were beside the river of things temporal. If you are drifting down to the rapids, lay hold of the tree: if you are caught up in the world's love, lay hold of Christ. He for your sake entered into time, that you might win eternity; for by his entering into time he did not cease himself to be eternal.

The tree of life, the cross, stands beside the river of time. Its fruits fall to those who receive the messiah's gift of eternity passing into time, so that temporal creatures may pass out of it. This is the eschatological victory of timelessness over time. Here we find Augustine's only stab at a solution to the problem of temporality. The endurance of awareness, the scriptural articulations of history, and the moment of conversion are but stop-gap measures. Even after reckoning with Augustine's insights in the *Confessions*, the *City of God*, and the *Gift of Perseverance*, we are left open to the threat of time. All we can do is wait for the wood of the tree of life to provide the kindling for the fires to come.

The Revolutionary *Kairos*

Augustine left us dragged along by the river of time, whereas Agamben hints we might master time by transforming ourselves into clocks of increasingly refined ingenuity. But the river and the clock meet in the messiah. If we look back to Agamben's earlier work, such as *Infancy and History*, it is obvious that a polemic against ordinary time drives his messianism. Ordinary time means a "homogeneous, empty time," as Walter Benjamin (2007: 13.260) put it in his theses on history. For Martin Heidegger (1962: 65.377), ordinary time was "a pure sequence of 'nows,' without beginning and without end." Heidegger (1962: 79.462) further clarified that this nefarious temporality consisted in a "continuously enduring sequence of pure 'nows.'" Both Benjamin and Heidegger anathematize any representation of time as a line divisible into geometrical points. This accounts for their shared appeal in the estimation of Agamben, who repudiates mathematized temporality. "Lived time is represented through a metaphysical-geometric concept (the discrete point or instant)," writes Agamben (2007: 110) in his attack on temporal quantification, "and it is then taken as if this concept were itself the real time of experience." This misappropriation of temporality results in confusion between time and the timeless, leading to humankind's fundamental alienation from its own temporal condition. As the clock ticks away the hours of our workday, we dream that it dictates the time of our lives. "The 'nows' are what get counted," wrote Heidegger (1962: 81.437). "The world-time which is 'sighted' in this manner in the use of clocks, we call the 'now-time' [*Jetzt-zeit*]." For Agamben (2007: 101–2, 107), the mathematized now of the clock manifested the empty now, which bears no particular content and lacks any inherent meaning.

Heidegger's student Karl Löwith (1949: 204–7) located the origin of this empty concept of time in Christian Neoplatonism. Agamben (2007: 102) retells Löwith's story, arguing that Christianity absorbed the Aristotelian notion of "a quantified and infinite continuum of precise fleeting instants." Rather than subjecting this continuum to a Stoic cycle, Christian thinkers flattened it out into the linear process of salvation history. This is how Agamben reads Augustine. "While the classical representation of time is a circle, the image guiding the Christian conceptualization of it is a straight line," Agamben (2007: 103) writes, adding that, in "contrast with the directionless time of the classical world, this time has a direction and a purpose." The false cycles of the polytheists are disrupted by the straight route of Christ. Agamben (2007: 103–4) cannot help but attribute the circle-line dichotomy to the Augustinian tradition: "The whole of the eleventh book of Augustine's *Confessions*, with its anguished and unresolved interrogation of fleeting time, shows that continuous, quantified time has not been abolished, [but] simply displaced from the paths of the stars to interior duration." Augustinian temporality, however, continues to operate on the level of cosmological time, not just that of psychological interiority. By no means is it merely subjective. The happy outcome is that Augustine's account of time can still be useful for those of us who feel alienated by the forty-hour working week.

The secular time of the industrial world is for Agamben merely Greco-Christian time robbed of any resolution. "The modern concept of time," writes Agamben (2007: 105), "is a secularization of rectilinear, irreversible Christian time, albeit sundered from any notion of end and emptied of any other meaning but that of a structured process in terms of before and after." Such a chronology is better suited to the mechanisms of manufacturing than to the reality of human life. Agamben (2007: 105) calls this "dead time," which "characterizes life in modern cities and factories," seeming to "give credence to the idea that the precise fleeting instant is the only human time." Instead of an eschatological climax, we await the cues of wage-labor. De-sacralized, punch-clock linearity gives rise to the crudest of progress narratives. Pinker's *Enlightenment Now* is only one of the latest and most egregious examples. Against this, Agamben argues that the dead emptiness of ordinary time must be overcome by a fuller conception of time. But this fulfillment of temporality has to face up to the problem of the present as Augustine encountered it. "Any attempt to conceive of time differently," writes Agamben (2007: 110), "must inevitably come into conflict with this concept [of the now-point], and a critique of the instant is the logical condition for a new experience of time."

Throughout *Infancy and History*, Agamben lays out the stakes of the problem of the present for both philosophy and politics. Invoking Benjamin, he warns us that ordinary time lurks even within revolutionary politics. To achieve revolutionary change, it is not enough to re-write history. Time itself must be altered. "Every conception of history is invariably accompanied by a certain experience of time which is implicit in it, conditions it, and thereby has to be elucidated," writes Agamben (2007: 99), adding that the "original task of a genuine revolution, therefore, is never merely to 'change the world,' but also, and above all, to change time."

Humankind has fallen prey to a strange tension between its sense of time and its sense of history. At any given time, we feel trapped in the moment or drawn inexorably into the future. We either live only for the next instant or remain dormant in the face of historical determinism. This is the "fundamental contradiction of modern man," according to Agamben (2007: 99). The solution, in his view, must be a new philosophy of time constructed in conversation with post-Marxist historical materialism. That is what makes Agamben's approach ultimately more indebted to Benjamin than to Heidegger.

Benjamin's terse theses on history are packed with insights into the political and theological baggage weighing down humankind's historical consciousness. Each thesis contains within itself the seed of an idea that Agamben takes entire books to develop. In his thirteenth thesis, for example, Benjamin (2007: 13.260–1) explicitly links the illusion of "historical progress" to society's "progression through a homogeneous, empty time." Rather than succumbing to this delusion, he warns his readers to adopt a concept of the historical moment that is full of meaning, not unlike Paul's messianic *kairos*. "History," wrote Benjamin (2007: 14.161), "is the subject of a structure whose site is not homogenous, empty time, but time filled by the presence of the now." This *Jetztzeit* is the pleroma that makes past injustices present, thereby amplifying the demand placed by history's victims on those who are still alive. Old ways of thinking about time, says Benjamin (2007: A.263), must be replaced by "a conception of the present as the 'time of the now' which is shot through with chips of Messianic time." The concrete manifestation of this new conception could consist in the institution of a revolutionary calendar or the firing of cannons at clocktowers, making it seem like time had stopped and political clarity had been attained in the revolutionary present (Benjamin 2007: 15.261–2). Just as the sun stopped in the sky so that Joshua could win his battle (Josh. 10:1–15), the clocks crumble and the river halts in Benjamin's messianic moment.

Augustine would applaud Benjamin's skepticism in the face of the progress narratives we tell ourselves in this *saeculum*. He might also be amenable to Benjamin's evocative image of the angel of history, rooted in the interpretation of a painting by Paul Klee. As Benjamin (2007: 9.257–8) describes the angelic figure:

His face is turned toward the past. Where we perceive a chain of events, he sees one single catastrophe which keeps piling wreckage and hurls it in front of his feet. The angel would like to stay, awaken the dead, and make whole what has been smashed. But a storm is blowing in from Paradise; it has got caught in his wings with such a violence that the angel can no longer close them. The storm irresistibly propels him into the future to which his back is turned, while the pile of debris before him grows skyward. This storm is what we call progress.

The angel of history is fundamentally retrospective. Forced into the future without being able to see where he is going, he can only look backward. It is as if he were undergoing Augustinian *distentio*. Augustine likewise shares Benjamin's sense that the eschatological arrival of justice will retroactively highlight the obscure boundaries between virtue and vice as they have appeared to us. The supposed vices of those who appear to be losing (in the grand scheme of economic history, for example) will be shown to be forgotten virtues, as the prosperity gospel is turned on its head. The humor and cunning of the vagabond shall be revealed to be the strength of the people. Characteristics like these "have retroactive force," writes Benjamin (2007: 4.255), adding that "as flowers turn toward the sun, by dint of a secret heliotropism the past strives to turn toward that sun which is rising in the sky of history."

Similarities between Augustine and Benjamin can in part be explained by the fact they are both eschatological thinkers. This does not mean, however, that they agree on how the eschatological future relates to the past and present. Augustine is skeptical about the capacity of the present to bear the breadth of political significance with which Benjamin insists we must burden it. The latter's historical materialist outlook further grants him a certain appreciation of historical meaning that remains closed to Augustine, whose view is closer to what Benjamin characterizes as the ancient Jewish resistance to soothsayers claiming knowledge about the future. In that case, as Benjamin (2007: B.264) concludes, humility in the face of the future did not necessarily demand that "the future turned into homogeneous, empty time. For every second of time was the strait gate through which the Messiah might enter." Augustine's messiah, however, had already arrived (for the first time, at least). From the vantage point of the Christ-event, the future did indeed seem to have turned into homogeneous, empty time.

Agamben wants to get back behind Augustine's post-messianic time by re-engaging Paul's not-yet-Christian messianism and re-activating Benjamin's call for a revolutionary temporality dependent not upon the present as a mathematical point, but upon the now as a moment of action. Agamben (2007: 99) is adamant that the "vulgar representation of time as a precise and homogeneous continuum" renders us powerless. Ordinary time hides transformative potential behind an impersonal continuum. Mixing Heidegger's *Being and Time* (*Sein und Zeit*) into his reading of Benjamin, Agamben (2007: 113) preaches authentic temporality against the dull thud of public time's pendulum:

[T]he originality of *Sein und Zeit* is that the foundation of historicity takes place in tandem with an analysis of temporality which elucidates a different and more authentic experience of time. At the heart of this experience there is no longer the precise, fleeting instant throughout linear time, but the moment of the authentic decision in which *Dasein* experiences its own finiteness, which at every moment extends from birth to death ...

For Agamben, the chance for change lies in this appropriation of temporality as one's own. Ownership of time commences with the move from the present as a mathematical limit to the now as a lived experience.

Only by rethinking time in terms of such a moment, says Agamben (2007: 114–15), can humankind recover its primordial experience of time as "pleasure." Recasting time as pleasure undercuts the old distinction between time's emptiness and eternity's fullness. This strange new hedonism constitutes a third way, leading us out of alienation via the recognition that we are at home in time. Time is not our prison, but our salvation, according to Agamben (2007: 115):

For history is not, as the dominant ideology would have it, man's servitude to continuous linear time, but man's liberation from it: the time of history and the *kairos* in which man, by his initiative, grasps favourable opportunity and chooses his own freedom in the moment. Just as the full, discontinuous, finite, and complete time of pleasure must be set against the empty, continuous, and infinite time of vulgar historicism, so the chronological time of pseudo-history must be opposed by the kairological time of authentic history.

Agamben here combines most explicitly the messianic present of Benjamin's political theology and Paul's "time of the now" (*ho nun kairos*). As a corollary, Paul must be distanced from the empty timeline of homogeneous Christian history. He must be sundered from the *saeculum*. The guilt instead lies with those Agamben (2007: 105) calls the "Neoplatonizing patristics," who imported too much mathematically inflected philosophizing into their dry chronology, which lent itself more to despair than pleasure. Augustine's anxieties over *distentio* and belatedness in the *Confessions* stand accused. Kairology, conversely, aims to nullify our lamentations about being stuck in time. The *kairos* strikes when the time is ripe for our initiative. It explodes out of the homogeneous continuum with revolutionary fervor. Agamben (2007: 115) describes revolutionary kairology as follows:

> It is this time which is experienced in authentic revolutions, which, as Benjamin remembers, have always been lived as a halting of time and an interruption of chronology. But a revolution from which there springs not a new chronology, but a qualitative alteration of time (a kairology), would have the weightiest consequence and would alone be immune to absorption into the reflux of restoration. He who... has remembered history as he would remember his original home, will bring this memory to everything, *will exact this promise from each instant*: he is the true revolutionary and the true seer, released from time not at the millennium, but *now*.

The now is the site of liberation. Discarding the precise instant in favor of a moment of decision, humankind can come to master temporality, exacting promises from it as if it were a political prisoner. Reversing the lamentation of time's power over us, kairology puts time at our mercy.

In *The Time That Remains*, Agamben pushes his fusion of Benjamin's present and Paul's "now-time" to its breaking point. The goal, says Agamben (2005: 62), is to arrive at a temporality that is "neither chronological time nor the apocalyptic eschaton." He hopes to find it in the *kairos sunestalmenos* of 1 Cor. 7:29-31, which he interprets not as the end of time, but as the contraction of time. If Agamben were producing a film about Paul, it would be a suspenseful thriller rather than an apocalyptic blockbuster. The time is getting short, but this does not mean we are on the cusp of timelessness. Instead it signals that each moment matters more than ever. Messianic time therefore remains time, even as it opens *chronos* up to the possibility of *kairos*. "What we take hold of when we seize *kairos* is not another time," writes Agamben (2005: 69), "but a contracted and abridged *chronos*." While *The Time That Remains* maintains its focus squarely on Paul, historical materialism has not entirely receded from the scene. Benjamin, according to Agamben (2005: 143), had endowed his term *Jetztzeit* "with the same qualities as those pertaining to the *ho nun kairos* in Paul's paradigm of messianic time." Across two millennia, from the first century to the twentieth, *kairos* continues to name the seizure that grasps time from within for the purposes of human transformation. Far from the naïve moment of popular mindfulness, Agamben's instant is the fulfillment of unfulfilled *chronos* through the institution of a meaningful present.

Kairological time can fill any present moment with a messianic *pleroma*. The messiah does not belong only to the future, let alone to the past. Each instant, writes Agamben (2005: 76), can be identified as "the messianic now, and the messianic is not the chronological end of time, but the present as the exigency of fulfilment." The Pauline logic of *kairos* and *pleroma*, interpreted in Agamben's terms rather than Augustine's, is what enables us to appropriate time for ourselves and thereby emancipate ourselves from the false fetters of linear temporality. Our enslavement to time, which drove Augustine to sorrow, was the result of misrecognition. To escape, all we need is a slight but decisively messianic shift in perspective. *Chronos* dreamed itself our master, but now we know better. The messiah has come; we are liberated. This very moment is the narrow door through which the messiah's transformative presence is passing. There is therefore nothing to lament. We need only knock and the secrets of historical time will be opened to us.

The Devil's Breakfast

On Augustinian grounds, the idea that we could master time by investing the present moment with meaning remains a dangerously proud presumption. Living within the *saeculum* as we do, the linearity of time should indeed strike us as empty of obvious significance. Just as the Son emptied Himself out to become incarnate, so the *saeculum* has undergone a kind of kenosis.

Augustine's dim view of our days can only be brightened by the illumination of Scripture. In its pages alone can we find something like the beginning and the end of the story. We may never be able to fill in this era's gaps; nevertheless, we can orient ourselves toward an absolute beginning and an absolute end. Chronologically speaking, that would mean the cosmic spring of Genesis 2 and the eschaton foreshadowed in the New Testament. Yet this relative legibility of Scripture fails to render the political fits and starts of our age any more legible, since the extreme bookends of cosmological time cannot serve as indices of historical time as we live through it. Secular science says something similar: the big bang and the entropic heat-death of the universe do not tell us whether a rebellion would be justified or not. If we fail to appreciate this gap between cosmic and historical speculation, suggests Augustine, we risk deluding ourselves by bringing pseudo-eschatological clarity into the present. The points of creation and the eschaton are, as Löwith (1949: 168–9) once wrote, "supra-historical," making history as we know it little more than an "interim between the past disclosure of its sacred meaning and its future fulfillment." Augustine's reticence to weaponize the Pauline rhetoric of the *kairos* for present political purposes is what has led to his reputation in some circles as a quietist.

Near the end of *City of God* 17, Augustine aims to clarify his stance on eschatological timing by interpreting an unexpected passage from Scripture: Eccl. 10:16. "'Woe to the land whose king is a child and whose princes eat in the morning,'" it says, according to the *Vetus Latina* edition available in North Africa in the early fifth century. "'Blessed is the land whose king is the son of nobles and whose princes eat at the proper time, in strength, not in confusion'" (CD 17.20).[1] Augustine does not hesitate to associate the son of nobles with Christ, leaving Satan to play the role of the devilish child-king. Their respective kingdoms correspond to the heavenly and earthly cities as eschatological categories. The earthly city houses those who will have turned out to be reprobates, while the citizens of the heavenly city are the predestined elect. Curiously enough, here the cities are distinguished not just on account of God's timeless decision, but also with reference to their own timing. As Augustine (CD 17.20) writes:

> The princes of the devil's city dine "in the morning," that is, before the proper hour, since they are not awaiting the opportune happiness that truly is in the age to come. Instead, they rush ahead, wanting to be blessed by fame in this age. But the princes of the city of Christ wait patiently for the time of the happiness that is not false.[2]

The devil's breakfast feasts on false certainty. By trying to drag eschatological clarity back into our own time, Satan's princes use worldly fame and happiness to lure humankind toward an embrace of emptiness. Agamben's enemy is the homogeneous emptiness of the timeline; Augustine's enemy is the sinister emptiness occasioned by the illusion that we are living in some unique *kairos* of bounty and opportunity. As the earlier books of the *City of God* attest, present gains count for nothing next to the timeless security of the eternal. The devil is a liar. According to Augustine, the proper stance is not a forced seizure of the present in the name of the future, but humble awaiting of the future itself.

The devil's breakfast must, then, be avoided at all costs. Augustine knew this in the fifth century, but many others have also figured it out over the past 1,600 years. In his pamphlet *News Out of Purgatory*, written around 1590, a Shakespearean-era jack of all trades named Richard Tarlton recounted the hypocritical complaints of a pudding-loving vicar who used his homily to attack those who dared to dine before receiving the Eucharist at Sunday mass. "Oh neighbours," cried the clergyman (Belfield 1978: 317), "as I came this day to churchward, I came into a house, nay into an alehouse, where I found a crew at breakfast before mass, at a bloody breakfast, a black breakfast, yea, neighbours, a devil's breakfast!" The joke is that the vicar knew this damning fact because he too was in the damnable alehouse before heading to say mass that morning. Beneath the joke lies the truth that hastening to seize the day (even the Lord's day) before the time is risky business for clerics and crews alike. Just as premature breakfasts can ruin an otherwise salvific morning, so can we be ruined by premature attempts to disentangle the hidden threads of history before all is said and done. Seeking a rational diagnosis of historical time, we are likely to cast ourselves further down into diabolical confusion. If we break the fast of the *saeculum*, we should expect a kind of demonic indigestion. Taking Ecclesiastes into consideration, it would seem wisest to leave the feast for later.

The fact that time remains empty for Augustine does not, however, make change impossible. His arguments do not aim to silence political debate (as if any arguments could). Throughout his life, Augustine was constantly engaged in the political strife of his era. The debates into which he entered lurk between the lines of his writings on time and history. We cannot understand Augustine if we refuse to reckon with his turn away from the Manichaean cosmos, his resistance to Donatist puritanism, or his scorn for the Pelagian propaganda preaching that we can pull ourselves up by our own bootstraps. Sometimes, as in his Epistle 93, written around 408 CE to the Donatist-affiliated leader Vincentius, Augustine would even counsel the use of physical force to change material situations on the ground for the sake of peace and unity in the African Christian community. His philosophy of time did not, then, preclude him from participating in politics. He was never really a quietist. Merely observing this fact does not succeed in adequately squaring Augustine's account of temporality with the facts of his political engagement. Agamben's suspicion that the notion of empty time might inhibit our political imaginations retains its force. If we seek a more satisfying rejoinder to that suspicion, we must turn to one last modern debate, which will shed light on the long afterlife of Augustinian temporality as a politically motive force.

In the middle of the twentieth century, the political theology of time became the subject of dispute between Malcolm X and Martin Luther King, Jr. Both were, in their own distinct ways, equally steeped in politics and theology; both grasped the practical fact that how we think about time matters for how we engage with the possibility for sociopolitical change. Malcolm's theology was forged in his journey through the Nation of Islam toward an eventual universalism rooted in the brotherhood of all Muslims regardless of race or nationality. The *umma* was his destiny. Nevertheless, his approach to time was deeply rooted in the exigencies of the political situation he faced: namely, the oppression of his fellow Black Americans in both the Jim Crow south and the hypocritical northern cities. The urgency of the demand placed upon Malcom by his own era can be keenly felt in "The Ballot or the Bullet," a speech which he delivered in slightly varying versions on at least two occasions. On April 3, 1964, he spoke on the matter at Cory Methodist Church in Cleveland; on April 12, 1964, he ploughed anew the same ground before a Baptist audience in Detroit. Having just split with the Nation, Malcolm was debuting a fresh persona, though his rhetoric retained its characteristic force. His recently founded organization, The Muslim Mosque, Inc., aimed to reformulate his emancipatory message in more explicitly universalizing terms by way of brand-new speeches, rallies, and street-level interventions. While this work began in Harlem, it soon spread as far afield as Ohio and Michigan, where he spoke specifically on the denial of voting rights to Black citizens. As the title of this particular talk would imply, Malcolm planned to leave his audience with the lingering sense that, if voting rights were to be ensured for all people, some kind of violent resistance might become necessary.

In the text of this speech, Malcolm reminds his readers that the time for political transformation is neither yesterday nor tomorrow, but now. The new mantra for the civil rights movement should run, according to Malcolm (1965: 32), as follows: "Give it to us now. Don't wait for next year. Give it to us yesterday, and that's not fast enough." In the Cleveland version of the speech, Malcolm (1965: 38) continued: "We want freedom now, but we're not going to get it saying 'We Shall Overcome.' We've got to fight until we overcome." Now is the time for action. Time, in this formulation, means not just any time, but the time for significant political change.

This is Malcolm's *kairos*. A meaningful engagement with time on these grounds requires an emphasis on the now, which Malcolm is happy to provide. Near the end of his Cleveland speech, Malcolm (1965: 44) pitches his words directly to the President of the United States of America: "If he's for civil rights, let him go into the Senate next week and declare himself. Let him go in there right now and declare himself... Let him go in there right now and take a moral stand: right now, not later." For those listening to Malcolm, and for President Lyndon B. Johnson alike, waiting was no longer an option. All the audience had to do was wake up and the battle would already be won.

Any advice to wait in the face of this present moment of decision would, in Malcolm's view, rob the Black community of the power over time it needs in order to take a stand. To conceive of temporality as empty or neutral would be to cut the legs out from under the emancipatory movement which Malcolm sought to further. What Agamben called dead time would lead to dead bodies in the streets. For Malcolm, however, time is very much alive. Time and truth stand on the side of the oppressed today. This use of the word "today" does not denote any particular date on the calendar. Its meaning transcends the way we check off days on our quotidian march through life. Malcolm's today was a today laden with the weight of political theology. While the full text of Malcolm's final speech, delivered at Columbia's Barnard College on February 19, 1965, has yet to be fully reconstructed, he was reported to have said it was (or is) a time for martyrs now. On February 21, 1965, two days after making that last remark, Malcolm X was gunned down.

Dr. King, meanwhile, offers a distinct approach to the political theology of time in his "Letter from Birmingham Jail," written in August 1963, about a year and a half before Malcolm's murder. In this letter, King responded to accusations leveled by White moderate preachers. They had complained that he was acting in an untimely fashion and thereby failing to await the mysteriously appointed time for the overcoming of racial oppression. King, however, argues that there is no need to adopt a messianic kairology in the present so as to ensure society's transformation. "I had hoped," writes King (2013: 178), "that the white moderate would reject the myth concerning time in relation to the struggle for freedom." This myth or this attitude, continued King (2013: 178), "stems from a tragic misconception of time, from the strangely irrational notion that there is something in the very flow of time that will inevitably cure all ills. Actually, time itself is neutral; it can be used either destructively or constructively." Here the emptiness of *chronos* becomes its power. Therefore, says King (2013: 178), "we must use time creatively, in the knowledge that the time is always ripe to do right." Malcolm and King thus agree that we should not wait too long for sociopolitical transformation, but their reasons for doing so are distinct. For Malcolm, it is because we must seize time in the now as a *kairos*; for King, it is because there is no special moment to seize in the first place. The absence of a *kairos* is what allows us to be ethical in time. A demythologized *chronos* turns out to be the time that we need.

To reframe King's approach in Augustinian phrasing: the chronological conditions of *distentio* and belatedness are perfectly hospitable to revolutionary upheaval in the face of social injustice. We find ourselves living within an empty, homogeneous, neutral timeline. Our emancipation can only take place along that same timeline. As Malcolm's words amply attest, the dream of a transformational *kairos* has lost little of its rhetorical punch, but the reality of such a *kairos* need not be presumed in order to realize the goal of emancipation. King's sensibility is reminiscent of a set of monastic regulations cited by Agamben in *The Highest Poverty*. Called the *Rule of the Master*, it was an anonymous collection of monastic regulations composed probably in the sixth century CE. In that context, the problem facing the monks (whose names we will never know) is what to do when nature itself conceals from us the movements by which we usually measure time. Luckily, there remains a solution (Agamben 2013: 20): "On a cloudy day, when the sun hides its rays from the earth, let the brothers, whether in the monastery or on the road or in the field, estimate elapsed time by careful calculation of the hours, and no matter what time it may be, the usual Office is to be said." When the clouds obscure the sun, the sun-dial does not work. When clocks are absent, we must become clocks unto ourselves. In either case, the possibility of political transformation does not disappear. Any time is good enough for a revolution.

Conclusion

Augustine has struck few of his readers as a revolutionary. This need not, however, make him a quietist. As King's political theology of time suggests, an empty view of temporality can give rise to the transformative upheaval of entire social systems. Augustine, as bishop of a not unimportant city, was constantly engaged in politics. Our interpretation of his approach to time should reflect his sociopolitical scenario, as well as the fact that his approach did not disappear along with its imperial context. "Christianity does not entail submission to the status quo," as the Marxist philosopher Andrew Collier (2001: 115) wrote. "Christianity is not an ideal theory," said the Dominican Herbert McCabe (1980: 164) in a similar spirit, "it is a praxis, a particular kind of challenge to the world." For McCabe (1980: 168), this practical force of Christianity means we must "look at the present from the perspective of the future." Augustine's account of temporal and historical change lives up to these lofty characterizations of the Christian tradition.

Still, Agamben's concerns about the emptiness of homogeneous chronology should not be dismissed out of hand. His position remains a formidable alternative to the Augustinian account of time. Nor can the rhetorical power animating certain passages of the Apostle Paul, Walter Benjamin, and Malcolm X be dismissed. Perhaps the ideal of revolution and the idea of a *kairos* will always be entangled to some degree. From an Augustinian point of view, however, there is bound to be something dangerously proleptic about any attempt to posit a *kairos* in the present. This is true of the present instant when it comes to the philosophy of time in the abstract. It is also true of the moment of conversion as it appears to punctuate the individual convert's life. And it is nowhere truer than in the case of political transformations taking place on a world-historical plane. The present point of the timeline vanishes before our eyes; the moment of decision is mad; and the joints of time remain hidden from us for the best of reasons.

Kairologically speaking, a revolution would have to be instantaneous, transformational, and ultimately unimaginable. Back in *Confessions* 8, Augustine cast conversion as the radical turning-point for an individual. It named the moment when a person becomes someone or something else. We seem to be able to make sense of a person's life before or after conversion, but the hinge around which the moment of conversion swings is concealed. Moving to the scale of an entire political society, the same logic holds for a revolution. We cannot really know the right time for it. We might think its appointed time is upon us and be entirely mistaken. Nor can we look past this point of transformation in order to see precisely how things will fall into place after the event. Even Marx would admit that divining the post-revolutionary order in advance is a fool's errand. It would be like trying to gaze back behind creation or ahead beyond the eschaton. Our tendency to presume that change takes place in a choppy, instantaneous manner continues to create impasses for our political imaginations. That, in the end, is the appeal of the political theology of time we find in Augustine of Hippo and Martin Luther King, Jr. Despite the tendency of certain observers to decry both figures as quietists, falling silent in the face of injustice, they were actively engaged in the process of political change. Neither, however, held that such change could be produced only by humankind's willful seizure of temporality for its own purposes. The homogeneous river of time flows on, but it is not as empty as some have supposed. It is full of possibilities, even if those possibilities creep up on us unawares, with the result that we only notice they have become actualities in retrospect. An Augustinian timeframe leaves copious amounts of room for an activism beyond quietism. The time always was and always will be ripe to do right.

Conclusion

This Life's Future

In his 2019 book *This Life*, the philosophically minded scholar of comparative literature Martin Hägglund argues that time is all we have. As temporally finite beings, our first task must be to reconcile ourselves to the fact that we will never slip out of the constraints of temporality. The dream of existence beyond time has led us only in the direction of philosophical, political, and even economic misconceptions. Envisioning God and heaven as timeless in the strict sense distracts us from the role played by time in conditioning every aspect of who we are. Juxtaposing time to a timeless eternity, as Augustine does, would then have the effect of distorting humankind's understanding of itself and its own possibilities. Hägglund seeks to fix the situation by ridding us of our divine delusions. As the *New Yorker* review of his book puts it: "If God is dead, your time is everything" (Wood 2019).

Hägglund's work provides a welcome rejoinder to suspiciously sanguine accounts of the state of the world, such as the progress-mad visions we encountered in Steven Pinker's *Enlightenment Now*. According to Hägglund, things are not getting better. The Enlightenment did not kick-start an era of ceaseless economic and technological betterment which only the sourest of intellectuals could fail to appreciate. This is not to say that Hägglund positions himself against all Enlightenment or post-Enlightenment figures. On the contrary, his worldview has been deeply influenced by a litany of modern thinkers, from Hegel and Marx to Derrida and

King. His embrace of a Marxist framework differs from Agamben's adaptation of Benjamin's historical materialism, though it is just as committed to social change. Fittingly, the second half of *This Life* lays out a program for addressing the injustices of our world by drawing upon the teachings of these figures in order to make way for a "secular faith," which alone could open up "the possibility of our spiritual freedom" (Hägglund 2019: 36).

The difference between Pinker and Hägglund is not simply one of political affiliation. While the former is Whiggish in his progress-minded centrism and the latter is Marxian in his call for full-scale social transformation, their real discrepancy lies in their attitudes toward time. Pinker writes as if he were the master of time cosmological, psychological, and historical. Time's trajectory is as easy as the stock market for him to track statistically. Hägglund, however, grasps temporality on a more fundamental level. Like Augustine, he wants to bear witness to the true power wielded by time over our lives. His political project is not solely rooted in a sober appraisal of the socioeconomic state of global affairs. Instead, the philosophy of time governs his desire for political change.

Hägglund (2019: 27) offers "a secular vision of why *everything depends on what we do with our time together*" (original emphasis). What he is striving to make clear is his sense that political engagement becomes all the more pressing once we acknowledge that there is no life for us outside time. The importance of time increases in direct opposition to that of eternity. If many of us in the twenty-first century can no longer wrap our heads around the idea of something timeless, let alone desire the eternal above the temporal, this is no tragedy. The elevation of eternity at the expense of the temporal world was a bewitching illusion. Hägglund departs radically from the Augustinian worldview, which always balanced its obsession with time with a reverence for timeless eternity.

Rejecting the eternal allows Hägglund to treat this temporal world as an end in itself. One strange consequence of this strategy is that it brings him back closer to Pinker's otherwise dissimilar approach, insofar as he too must now entertain the possibility of historical progress.

Whereas Pinker saw progress as chugging along like a well-oiled machine and Augustine repudiated our desire to posit progress in history as we live through it, Hägglund's progress is akin to Marx's maxim about the power of philosophy to change the world.

According to Hägglund (2019: 399), democratic socialism is the goal and the future is how we get there:

Needless to say, there is no guarantee that we will succeed in achieving democratic socialism. Even if we do succeed, it may take more generations than we would like to imagine. What I have sought to show is that we can get there—that we can recognize the principles of democratic socialism as our own commitments, that we can make sense of life beyond capitalism—and that there is never time to wait.

For Pinker, the current state of the world is so good that it barely needs changing. For Hägglund, things are so bad that global transformation now appears to be the only morally defensible option. Neither author can resist the temptation of diagnosing the present moment with quasi-scientific certainty. Augustine, however, would caution us to refrain from the presumption that the state of the world is something we can diagnose with an instantaneous value-judgment. The result would not be quietism, but it would be radically humble. As the life and writings of Martin Luther King, Jr., made so painfully clear, humility does lend itself to political mobilization. Whether Dr. King would agree more with Augustine or with Hägglund, who devoted the closing section of his book to a secularized appropriation of King's legacy, remains an open question.

At times, Hägglund does mention Augustine by name in his book, though his most salient criticisms have little to do with the finer points of the philosophy of time. Instead, he implies that Augustine was fundamentally incapable of having a healthy relationship with humane emotions like grief and desire. When Augustine's unnamed friend died back in *Confessions* 4, for example, he criticized himself for pouring his soul out on the sand by loving something temporary. To point your love in the direction of time-bound creatures is to engage in *cupiditas*: a warped form of desire that erroneously chases passing figments rather than clinging to what can never be lost. Hägglund (2019: 62) is particularly unimpressed with Augustine's self-criticism after he wept uncontrollably at the death of his own mother in *Confessions* 9. And yet, as Hägglund himself admits, this skepticism regarding the appropriateness of mourning is shared by many Christian authors. It is not the hallmark of Augustine alone.

When it comes to Augustine's account of temporality in *Confessions* 11, Hägglund proves an attentive reader. The death of the present does not escape his notice. As "you grasp the present moment, it is already ceasing to be," Hägglund (2019: 70) explains, adding that this "is not to say that the experience of time is an illusion. On the contrary, it is at work in everything you do." Trapped in time and pulled apart by *distentio*, we are forced to live under conditions quite different from those of an eternal God. Belatedness names those conditions. Hägglund (2019: 88–9) also notes the belated character of time-consciousness as explained by Augustine, which stands in contrast to a timeless deity who never runs late. Perhaps too quickly, Hägglund (2019: 71–2) links Augustine's account of temporal experience to the framing of our world as "secular." While we might expect Hägglund to pillory Augustine's discussion of the secular, he instead admits that what he is after is an Augustinian sense of faith in the *saeculum* itself. Just as Agamben sought to adapt Pauline messianism for the needs of modern revolution, Hägglund wants to decouple the form of a faith-commitment from its otherworldly connotations in Augustine. This is how Augustine, in spite of himself, aids Hägglund in the formulation of a secular faith capable of triggering political transformation.

Ultimately, despite his appreciation for Augustine's subtle engagement with time, Hägglund is unable to accept the Augustinian focus on eternity, which he sees as undermining any hope we have of fruitfully engaging with temporal life. After leveling criticism at Augustine, *This Life* attacks the entire Buddhist tradition for likewise denigrating temporality. "By subscribing to the value of absolute permanence," writes Hägglund (2019: 81), "Buddhism devalues everything that is impermanent." If we recall the careful work of scholars like Georges Dreyfus, we will be reminded that this is a grotesque oversimplification of the many philosophical accounts of time offered up by Buddhist authors over the past 2,500 years.

Buddhaghosa, who paid careful attention to the role played by memory in helping us achieve a healthy relationship with the temporal world, would not recognize himself in Hägglund's words. The virulence with which Hägglund pursues his vision of an embrace of this-worldly existence may, in the final appraisal, have led him to devalue contributions made by the Christian and Buddhist traditions to the philosophy of time upon which he draws.

In seeking to overcome this Augustinian (and supposedly Buddhist) anxiety over temporal life, Hägglund's approach becomes vaguely reminiscent of Agamben, who told us we must think of ourselves as originally at home in time, rather than alienated from it. Time is not pain but pleasure. This could be accomplished by allowing ourselves to desire even the most fleeting of diversions or better planning our days so that not a minute is wasted. But such interventions remain minor. To fully implement the alteration in time-consciousness suggested by Agamben and Hägglund would require revolutionary upheaval. Both authors are optimistic about the prospects for a revolution of this type.

Augustine, for his part, is not so sanguine. Temporal experience is characterized by an alienation impossible to overcome before the end of time. Only the eschaton can save us. Nevertheless, Augustine's temporal realism militates against the notion that he unthinkingly devalues time. While disproportionate affection for passing pleasures sets him ill at ease, he is equally uncomfortable with the idea that we ourselves could step outside the river of time and seize something timeless by our own initiative. That is why the mindfulness movement's talking point about every moment being an island of fulfillment finds no support in Augustine's writings. The future will always come along to frustrate our dreams of grasping eternity in the present and reverberate us back into the past. For now, then, time is indeed all we have, as much for Augustine as for Hägglund.

The bishop of Hippo is, however, far more skeptical than Hägglund or Agamben are about our ability to master the time in which we live. Transformation remains possible, but the changes the future brings reach us in a state of temporal vulnerability, thanks to the wound left upon our souls by the force of time as *distentio*. This wound finds its symptom in our sense of belatedness relative to turning-points both personal and historical. Despite appearances, neither conversions nor revolutions take place in an instant. Instead of instantaneous clarity, Augustine leaves us with an open-ended question. This is not just any question. It is the question that we are. Let us all say with Augustine (CF 4.4.9): "I have become a great question to myself." The truth about who and what we are will be revealed later. Until then, the question is not how we will overcome time, but how we will learn to live humbly within the time we are given.

Neither Hägglund nor Agamben has lived up to the Augustinian philosophy of time. We may need to look elsewhere for an interlocutor who can speak to our own era. The best candidate is the novelist and essayist Toni Morrison. Before she passed away in the summer of 2019, Morrison engaged ceaselessly with humankind's temporal experience in her writings. While her focus often fell upon groups facing exceptional injustices on the basis of gender and race, her literary exploration of these groups and their experiences revealed something about the temporal condition in general. She herself felt the crunch of the clock of industrial time more keenly than almost anyone. A working single mother, Morrison was reputed to have done most of her writing before the crack of dawn, since she had to spend the rest of the day performing wage labor and caring for her children.

In a 1996 lecture, Morrison laid bare her account of temporality. The title of her talk, "The Future of Time," indicated her desire to make sense of how we relate to our own future possibilities. In her view, the problem is that we, like Benjamin's angel of history, are overwhelmed by the amassed tragedy of our own shared past. In addition to the fact that history is a heap of unsettling atrocities, Morrison notes we can feel dwarfed by the immensity of geological and astronomical time-scales. Like Augustine and the Manichaeans, she too set the problem of time within its properly cosmological framework. Once we start thinking in terms of millions and billions of years, we experience a strain of chronological claustrophobia. Our meager plans for the future become constrained to the next few decades. We lose our taste for longer futures fueled by hope.

Morrison's cure for millennial malaise stands in stark contrast to Hägglund's, despite the fact that they share a segment on the political spectrum. Unlike him, she rejects the argument that religious perspectives and sacred literature have no beneficial role to play in helping us understand our temporal predicament. As Morrison (1996: 2) puts it:

Where there will be no Messiah, where afterlife is understood to be medically absurd, where the concept of an "indestructible soul" is not only unbelievable but increasingly unintelligible in intellectual and literate realms, where passionate, deeply held religious belief is associated with ignorance at best, violent intolerance at its worst, in times as suspicious of eternal life as these are, when "life in history supplants life in eternity," the eye, in the absence of resurrected or reincarnated life, becomes trained on the biological span of a single human being.

The resulting emphasis on immanence (and imminence) aims to be emancipatory, but it could lead to the opposite outcome, which Morrison (1996: 3) calls a "severely diminished future." Opting for an alternative stance would mean making room for a meditation on "deferral," not as the erasure of contemporary problems, but as an open-ended embrace of a future now scarcely imaginable. Morrison anticipates critics accusing her of peddling a new opiate for the masses. But she is not afraid "of being likened to missionaries who were accused of diverting their converts' attention from poverty during life to rewards following death" (Morrison 1996: 3). Her lack of fear is grounded in the sense that the sacred language of eternity, far from blinding us to our temporal condition, can help us better understand it.

By Morrison's lights, the fact that Augustine's account of time is framed in contrast to God's timeless eternity does not rule out its ability to instruct us and help us as we live out our temporal lives. The problem is not that certain religious authors, be they Christian or Buddhist, have pushed us to think beyond the constraints of time. The real problem, for Morrison (1996: 5), arises only "if religious language is discredited as contempt for the non-religious" or "if secular language bridles in fear of the sacred." That, she says, is when hope for the future is at its most fragile.

None of this means that Morrison is trying to sell her readers on yet another progress narrative. The subtlety of her treatment of time would doubtless escape the grasp of someone with a worldview like Pinker's. Hägglund's careful interpretation of Augustinian temporality, meanwhile, exonerates him from the worst of Morrison's charges. He does take the *tempora Christiana* seriously. His ultimate rejection of the Augustinian and Buddhist accounts of time, however, signals that he goes too far in his discrediting of the religious and his bridling of the sacred, all in the name of his own program of politically transformational progress.

Morrison (1996: 6), for her part, writes: "it isn't progress that interests me. I am interested in the future of time." When she talks about hope, she is not trumpeting baseless optimism in the face of the tragic, farcical form of history. Instead, says Morrison

(1996: 10), "I am detecting an informed vision based on harrowing experience that nevertheless gestures toward a redemptive future." She finds such visions of time in works written by authors who suffered historical violence motivated on the basis of gender, race, and colonialism. It is in those books and essays and poems, composed from a vantage point that offers little reason for hope, that Morrison (1996: 11) finds legitimate reason to believe that "time does have a future." Augustine would agree. The future, like the past, is more real than the present. Concerns like those voiced by Hägglund in *This Life* are real, but they need not lead us to erase religious literature from the history of the philosophy of time. Eternity's sacred intonations will still echo in our ears. All we need to do is let Augustine's lamentations of time and odes to the timeless add themselves to the chorus of the future.

NOTES

Introduction

1   CF 4.4.9: *factus eram ipse mihi magna quaestio.*

Chapter 1

1   CF 11.14.17: *duo ergo illa tempora, praeteritum et futurum,*
     quomodo sunt, quando et praeteritum iam non est et futurum
     nondum est? praesens autem si semper esset praesens nec in
     praeteritum transiret, non iam esset tempus, sed aeternitas. si ergo
     praesens, ut tempus sit, ideo fit, quia in praeteritum transit, quomodo
     et hoc esse dicimus, cui causa, ut sit, illa est, quia non erit, ut scilicet
     non vere dicamus tempus esse, nisi quia tendit non esse?
2   CF 11.15.20: *ecce praesens tempus, quod solum inveniebamus*
     longum appellandum, vix ad unius diei spatium contractum est.
     sed discutiamus etiam ipsum, quia nec unus dies totus est praesens.
     nocturnis enim et diurnis horis omnibus viginti quattuor expletur,
     quarum prima ceteras futuras habet, novissima praeteritas, aliqua
     vero interiectarum ante se praeteritas, post se futuras. et ipsa una
     hora fugitivis particulis agitur. quidquid eius avolavit, praeteritum
     est, quidquid ei restat, futurum.
3   CF 11.15.20: *si quid intellegitur temporis, quod in nullas iam vel*
     minutissimas momentorum partes dividi possit, id solum est quod
     praesens dicatur; quod tamen ita raptim a futuro in praeteritum
     transvolat, ut nulla morula extendatur. nam si extenditur, dividitur in
     praeteritum et futurum; praesens autem nullum habet spatium.
4   CF 11.16.21: *et tamen, domine, sentimus intervalla temporum et*
     comparamus sibimet et dicimus alia longiora et alia breviora.
5   CF 11.20.26: *nec futura sunt nec praeterita, nec proprie dicitur,*
     "tempora sunt tria, praeteritum, praesens, et futurum," sed fortasse
     proprie diceretur, "tempora sunt tria, praesens de praeteritis, praesens

de praesentibus, praesens de futuris." sunt enim haec in anima tria
quaedam et alibi ea non video, praesens de praeteritis memoria,
praesens de praesentibus contuitus, praesens de futuris expectatio.

6   CF 11.21.27: *praesens vero tempus quomodo metimur, quando non*
habet spatium? metitur ergo cum praeterit, cum autem praeterierit,
non metitur; quid enim metiatur non erit. sed unde et qua et quo
praeterit, cum metitur? unde nisi ex futuro? qua nisi per praesens?
quo nisi in praeteritum? ex illo ergo quod nondum est, per illud
quod spatio caret, in illud quod iam non est. quid autem metimur
nisi tempus in aliquo spatio?

7   CF 11.23.30: *ego scire cupio vim naturamque temporis, quo*
metimur corporum motus et dicimus illum motum verbi gratia
tempore duplo esse diuturniorem quam istum.

8   CF 11.26.33: *inde mihi visum est nihil esse aliud tempus quam*
distentionem; sed cuius rei, nescio, et mirum, si non ipsius animi.

9   CF 11.27.35: *ipsamque longam num praesentem metior, quando nisi*
finitam non metior? eius autem finitio praeteritio est: quid ergo est
quod metior? ubi est qua metior brevis? ubi est longa quam metior?
ambae sonuerunt, avolaverunt, praeterierunt, iam non sunt. et ego
metior fidenterque respondeo, quantum exercitato sensu fiditur, illam
simplam esse, illam duplam, in spatio scilicet temporis. neque hoc
possum, nisi quia praeterierunt et finitae sunt. non ergo ipsas quae
iam non sunt, sed aliquid in memoria mea metior, quod infixum
manet.

10   CF 11.28.37: *nam et expectat et attendit et meminit, ut id quod*
expectat per id quod attendit transeat in id quod meminerit. quis
igitur negat futura nondum esse? sed tamen iam est in animo
expectatio futurorum. et quis negat praeterita iam non esse? sed
tamen adhuc est in animo memoria praeteritorum. et quis negat
praesens tempus carere spatio, quia in puncto praeterit? sed tamen
perdurat attentio, per quam pergat abesse quod aderit.

11   CF 11.29.39: *ecce distentio est vita mea, et me suscepit dextera tua*
in domino meo, mediatore filio hominis inter te unum et nos multos,
in multis per multa, ut per eum apprehendam in quo et apprehensus
sum, et a veteribus diebus conligar sequens unum, praeterita oblitus,
non in ea quae futura et transitura sunt, sed in ea quae ante sunt [...].

12   CF 11.29.39: *non distentus sed extentus, non secundum*
distentionem sed secundum intentionem sequor ad palmam supernae
vocationis, ubi audiam vocem laudis et contempler delectationem
tuam nec venientem nec praetereuntem. nunc vero anni mei in
gemitibus, et tu solacium meum, domine, pater meus aeternus es.
at ego in tempora dissilui quorum ordinem nescio, et tumultuosis
varietatibus dilaniantur cogitationes meae, intima viscera animae
meae, donec in te confluam purgatus et liquidus igne amoris tui.

13 CF 4.4.9: *factus eram ipse mihi magna quaestio.*

14 CF 4.10.15: *nam quoquoversum se verterit anima hominis, ad dolores figitur alibi praeterquam in te, tametsi figitur in pulchris extra te et extra se. quae tamen nulla essent, nisi essent abs te. quae oriuntur et occidunt et oriendo quasi esse incipiunt, et crescunt ut perficiantur, et perfecta senescunt et intereunt: et non omnia senescunt, et omnia intereunt.*

15 CF 4.10.15: *ergo cum oriuntur et tendunt esse, quo magis celeriter crescunt ut sint, eo magis festinant ut non sint: sic est modus eorum. tantum dedisti eis, quia partes sunt rerum, quae non sunt omnes simul, sed decedendo ac succedendo agunt omnes universum, cuius partes sunt.*

16 CF 4.10.15: *eunt enim quo ibant, ut non sint, et conscindunt eam desideriis pestilentiosis, quoniam ipsa esse vult et requiescere amat in eis quae amat. in illis autem non est ubi, quia non stant: fugiunt, et quis ea sequitur sensu carnis? aut quis ea comprehendit, vel cum praesto sunt? tardus est enim sensus carnis, quoniam sensus carnis est: ipse est modus eius. sufficit ad aliud, ad quod factus est, ad illud autem non sufficit, ut teneat transcurrentia ab initio debito usque ad finem debitum. in verbo enim tuo, per quod creantur, ibi audiunt, "hinc" et "huc usque."*

17 CF 4.11.17: *quidquid per illam sentis in parte est, et ignoras totum cuius hae partes sunt, et delectant te tamen.*

18 CF 4.11.17: *sed si ad totum comprehendendum esset idoneus sensus carnis tuae, ac non et ipse in parte universi accepisset pro tua poena iustum modum, velles ut transiret quidquid existit in praesentia, ut magis tibi omnia placerent.*

19 CF 4.12.19: *non enim tardavit.*

20 CF 10.8.15: *nec ego ipse capio totum quod sum. ergo animus ad habendum se ipsum angustus est […]?*

21 CF 10.17.26: *quid ergo sum, deus meus? quae natura sum?*

22 CF 10.27.38: *sero te amavi, pulchritudo tam antiqua et tam nova, sero te amavi!*

23 CF 10.32.48: *ita mihi videor; forsitan fallar. sunt enim et istae plangendae tenebrae in quibus me latet facultas mea quae in me est, ut animus meus de viribus suis ipse se interrogans non facile sibi credendum existimet, quia et quod inest plerumque occultum est, nisi experientia manifestetur, et nemo securus esse debet in ista vita, quae tota temptatio nominatur, utrum qui fieri potuit ex deteriore melior non fiat etiam ex meliore deterior.*

24 CF 10.33.49: *sed delectatio carnis meae, cui mentem enervandam non oportet dari, saepe me fallit, dum rationi sensus non ita comitatur ut patienter sit posterior, sed tantum, quia propter illam*

meruit admitti, etiam praecurrere ac ducere conatur. ita in his pecco non sentiens et postea sentio.

25   CF 10.33.50: *tu autem, domine deus meus, exaudi: respice et vide et miserere et sana me, in cuius oculis mihi quaestio factus sum, et ipse est languor meus.*

26   CF 10.40.65: *neque in his omnibus quae percurro consulens te invenio tutum locum animae meae nisi in te.*

Chapter 2

1   CF 11.1.1: *tu prior voluisti ut confiterer tibi.*
2   CF 11.2.3: *confitear tibi quidquid invenero in libris tuis.*
3   CF 11.3.5: *audiam et intellegam quomodo in principio fecisti caelum et terram.*
4   CF 11.4.6: *ecce sunt caelum et terra! clamant quod facta sint; mutantur enim atque variantur. quidquid autem factum non est et tamen est, non est in eo quicquam quod ante non erat: quod est mutari atque variari. clamant etiam quod se ipsa non fecerint: "ideo sumus, quia facta sumus. non ergo eramus antequam essemus, ut fieri possemus a nobis."*
5   CF 11.5.7: *ergo dixisti et facta sunt atque in verbo tuo fecisti ea.*
6   CF 11.8.10: *utcumque video, sed quomodo id eloquar nescio, nisi quia omne quod esse incipit et esse desinit tunc esse incipit et tunc desinit, quando debuisse incipere vel desinere in aeterna ratione cognoscitur, ubi nec incipit aliquid nec desinit. ipsum est verbum tuum, quod et principium est, quia et loquitur nobis.*
7   CF 11.10.12: *quid faciebat deus antequam faceret caelum et terram?*
8   CF 11.11.13: *nondum intellegunt quomodo fiant quae per te atque in te fiunt, et conantur aeterna sapere, sed adhuc in praeteritis et futuris rerum motibus cor eorum volitat et adhuc vanum est. quis tenebit illud et figet illud, ut paululum stet, et paululum rapiat splendorem semper stantis aeternitatis, et comparet cum temporibus numquam stantibus, et videat esse incomparabilem, et videat longum tempus, nisi ex multis praetereuntibus motibus* [Verheijen amends this to *morulis*] *qui simul extendi non possunt, longum non fieri; non autem praeterire quicquam in aeterno, sed totum esse praesens; nullum vero tempus totum esse praesens; et videat omne praeteritum propelli ex futuro et omne futurum ex praeterito consequi, et omne praeteritum ac futurum ab eo quod semper est praesens creari et excurrere? quis tenebit cor hominis, ut stet et videat quomodo stans dictet futura et praeterita tempora nec futura nec praeterita aeternitas?*

9   CF 11.30.40: *videant itaque nullum tempus esse posse sine creatura.*

10 CF 11.31.41: *sed absit ut tu, conditor universitatis, conditor animarum et corporum, absit ut ita noveris omnia futura et praeterita. longe tu, longe mirabilius longeque secretius.*

11 CF 12.15.18: *expectatio rerum venturarum fit contuitus, cum venerint, idemque contuitus fit memoria, cum praeterierint: omnis porro intentio, quae ita variatur, mutabilis est …*

Chapter 3

1   CF 11.28.38: *et quod in toto cantico, hoc in singulis particulis eius fit atque in singulis syllabis eius, hoc in actione longiore, cuius forte particula est illud canticum, hoc in tota vita hominis, cuius partes sunt omnes actiones hominis, hoc in toto saeculo filiorum hominum, cuius partes sunt omnes vitae hominum.*

2   CD 1.35: *Meminerit sane in ipsis inimicis latere cives futuros, ne infructuosum vel apud ipsos putet, quod, donec perveniat ad confessos, portat infensos; sicut ex illorum numero etiam Dei civitas habet secum, quamdiu peregrinatur in mundo, conexos communione sacramentorum, nec secum futuros in aeterna sorte sanctorum …*

3   CD 1.35: *De correctione autem quorundam etiam talium multo minus est desperandum, si apud apertissimos adversarios praedestinati amici latitant, adhuc ignoti etiam sibi. Perplexae quippe sunt istae duae civitates in hoc saeculo invicemque permixtae, donec ultimo iudicio dirimantur; de quarum exortu et procursu et debitis finibus quod dicendum arbitror, quantum divinitus adiuvabor, expediam propter gloriam civitatis Dei, quae alienis a contrario comparatis clarius eminebit.*

4   CD 2.2: *Inde incidit quaestio, cur haec divina beneficia et ad impios ingratosque pervenerint, et cur illa itidem dura, quae hostiliter facta sunt, pios cum impiis pariter adflixerint? Quam quaestionem per multa diffusam (in omnibus enim cotidianis vel Dei muneribus vel hominum cladibus, quorum utraque indiscrete saepe accidunt, solet multos movere) ut pro suscepti operis necessitate dissolverem, aliquantum inmoratus sum …*

5   CD 2.21: *… vera autem iustitia non est nisi in ea re publica, cuius conditor rectorque Christus est, si et ipsam rem publicam placet dicere, quoniam eam rem populi esse negare non possumus.*

6   CD 2.22: *nemo conprehendit, iuste nemo reprehendit.*

7   CD 4.7: *Quis enim de hac re novit voluntatem Dei?*

8   CD 4.33: *Deus igitur ille felicitatis auctor et dator, quia solus est verus Deus, ipse dat regna terrena et bonis et malis, neque hoc*

temere et quasi fortuito, quia Deus est, non fortuna, sed pro rerum
ordine ac temporum occulto nobis, notissimo sibi; cui tamen ordini
temporum non subditus servit, sed eum ipse tamquam dominus regit
moderatorque disponit.

9 CD 5.8: *Qui vero non astrorum constitutionem, sicuti est cum*
quidque concipitur vel nascitur vel inchoatur, sed omnium
conexionem seriemque causarum, qua fit omne quod fit, fati
nomine appellant, non multum cum eis de verbi controversia
laborandum atque certandum est, quando quidem ipsum
causarum ordinem et quandam conexionem Dei summi tribuunt
voluntati et potestati, qui optime et veracissime creditur et cuncta
scire antequam fiant et nihil inordinatum relinquere …

10 CD 5.21: *valde superat vires nostras hominum occulta discutere*
et liquido examine merita diiudicare regnorum.

11 CD 5.26: *Haec ille secum et si qua similia, quae commemorare*
longum est, bona opera tulit ex isto temporali vapore cuiuslibet
culminis et sublimitatis humanae; quorum operum merces est aeterna
felicitas, cuius dator est Deus solis veraciter piis. Cetera vero vitae
huius vel fastigia vel subsidia, sicut ipsum mundum lucem auras,
terras aquas fructus ipsiusque hominis animam corpus, sensus
mentem vitam, bonis malisque largitur; in quibus est etiam quaelibet
imperii magnitudo, quam pro temporum gubernatione dispensat.

12 CR 22: *peractis ergo quinque aetatibus saeculi, quarum prima est ab*
initio generis humani, id est, ab adam, qui primus homo factus est,
usque ad noe, qui fecit arcam in diluuio, inde secunda est usque ad
abraham, qui pater electus est omnium quidem gentium, quae fidem
ipsius imitarentur; […] isti enim articuli duarum aetatum eminent in
ueteribus libris: reliquarum autem trium euangelio etiam declarantur,
cum carnalis origo domini iesu christi commemoratur. nam tertia est
ab abraham usque ad dauid regem: quarta a dauid usque ad illam
captiuitatem, qua populus dei in babyloniam transmigrauit: quinta
ab illa transmigratione usque ad aduentum domini nostri iesu christi;
ex cuius aduentu sexta aetas agitur.

13 CD 11.18: *Neque enim Deus ullum, non dico angelorum, sed vel*
hominum crearet, quem malum futurum esse praescisset, nisi pariter
nosset quibus eos bonorum usibus commodaret atque ita ordinem
saeculorum tamquam pulcherrimum carmen etiam ex quibusdam
quasi antithetis honestaret. Antitheta enim quae appellantur in
ornamentis elocutionis sunt decentissima, quae Latine ut appellentur
opposita, vel, quod expressius dicitur, contraposita.

14 CD 11.18: *Sicut ergo ista contraria contrariis opposita sermonis*
pulchritudinem reddunt, ita quadam non verborum, sed rerum
eloquentia contrariorum oppositione saeculi pulchritudo
componitur.

15   CD 11.21: *Neque enim eius intentio de cogitatione in cogitationem transit, in cuius incorporeo contuitu simul adsunt cunta quae novit; quoniam tempora ita novit nullis suis temporalibus notionibus, quem ad modum temporalia movet nullis suius temporalibus motibus.*

16   CD 11.23: *sicut pictura cum colore nigro loco suo posito, ita universitas rerum, si quis possit intueri, etiam cum peccatoribus pulchra est.*

17   CD 12.14: *Semel enim Christus mortuus est pro peccatis nostris.*

18   CD 16.12: *Nunc iam videamus procursum civitatis Dei etiam ab illo articulo temporis qui factus est in patre Abraham, unde incipit esse notitia eius evidentior, et ubi clariora leguntur promissa divina quae nunc in Christo videmus impleri.*

19   CD 16.43: *In quo* [i.e. David] *articulus quidam factus est et exordium quodam modo iuventutis populi Dei; cuius generis quaedam velut adulescentia ducebatur ab ipso Abraham usque ad hunc David. Neque enim frustra Matthaeus evangelista sic generationes commemoravit ut hoc primum intervallum quattuordecim generationibus commendaret, ab Abraham scilicet usque ad David. Ab adulescentia quippe incipit homo posse generare; propterea generationum ex Abraham sumpsit exordium; qui etiam pater gentium constitutus est, quando mutatum nomen accepit. Ante hunc ergo velut pueritia fuit huius generis populi Dei a Noe usque ad ipsum Abraham; et ideo in lingua inventa est, id est Hebraea. A pueritia namque homo incipit loqui post infantiam, quae hinc appellata est quod fari non potest. Quam profecto aetatem primam demergit oblivio, sicut aetas prima generis humani est deleta diluvio. Quotus enim quisque est, qui suam recordetur infantiam?*

20   CD 22.30: *Ipse etiam numerus aetatum, veluti dierum, si secundum eos articulos temporis computetur qui scripturis videtur expressi, iste sabbatismus evidentius apparebit, quoniam septimus invenitur.*

21   CD 13.20: *Sicut enim spiritus carni serviens non incongrue carnalis, ita caro spiritui serviens recte appellabitur spiritalis, non quia in spiritum convertetur, sicut nonnulli putant ex eo quod scriptum est: "Seminatur corpus animale, surget corpus spiritale," sed quia spiritui summa et mirabili obtemperandi facilitate subdetur usque ad implendam immortalitatis indissolubilis securissimam voluntatem, omni molestiae sensu, omni corruptibilitate et tarditate detracta.*

22   CD 15.24: *Sed huius Enoch translatio nostrae dedicationis est praefigurata dilatio. Quae quidem iam facta est in Christo, capite nostro, qui si resurrexit ut non moriatur ulterius, sed etiam ipse translatus est. Restat autem altera dedicatio universae domus cuius ipse Christusest fundamentum, quae differtur in finem, quando erit omnium resurrectio non moriturorum amplius.*

23   CD 18.49: *multi reprobi miscentur bonis et utrique tamquam in sagenam evangelicam colliguntur et in hoc mundo tamquam in mari utrique inclusi retibus indiscrete natant, donec perveniatur ad litus, ubi mali segregentur a bonis et in bonis tamquam in templo suo "sit Deus omnia in omnibus."*

24   CD 19.4: *Sicut ergo spe salvi, ita spe beati facti sumus, et sicut salutem, ita beatitudinem non iam tenemus praesentem, sed expectamus futuram, et hoc per patientiam …*

25   CD 19.10: *Sed neque sancti et fideles unius veri Dei summique cultores ab eorum fallaciis et multiformi temptatione securi sunt. In hoc enim loco infirmitatis et diebus malignis etiam ista sollicitudo non est inutilis, ut illa securitas, ubi pax plenissima atque certissima est, desiderio ferventiore quaeratur.*

26   CD 19.12: *Sic enim superbia perverse imitatur Deum. Odit namque cum sociis aequalitatem sub illo, sed inponere vult sociis dominationem suam pro illo. Odit ergo iustam pacem Dei et amat iniquam pacem suam.*

27   CD 19.13: *pax omnium rerum tranquillitas ordinis. Ordo est parium dispariumque rerum sua cuique loca tribuens dispositio. Proinde miseri, quia in quantum miseri sunt utique in pace non sunt, tranquillitate quidem ordinis carent, ubi perturbatio nulla est; verum tamen quia merito iusteque sunt miseri, in ea quoque ipsa misera sua praeter ordinem esse non possunt, non quidem coniuncti beatis, sed ab eis tamen ordinis lege seiuncti.*

28   CD 20.1: *Iste quippe dies iudicii proprie iam vocatur, eo quod nullus ibi erit inperitiae querellae locus cur iniustus ille sit felix et cur ille iustus infelix. Omnium namque tuncnonnisi bonorum vera et plena felicitas et omnium nonnisi malorum digna et summa infelicitas apparebit.*

29   CD 20.7: *Nec moveat quod saepe diabolus seducit etiam illos qui regenerati iam in Christo vias ingrediuntur Dei. "Novit" enim "Dominus qui sunt eius;"* [2 Tim. 2:19] *ex his in aeternam damnationem neminem ille seducit. Sic enim eos novit Dominus, ut Deus, quem nil latet etiam futurorum, non ut homo, qui hominem ad praesens videt (si tamen videt, cuius cor non videt), qualis autem postea sit futurus nec se ipsum videt.*

30   CD 20.14: *Quaedam igitur vis est intellegenda divina qua fiet ut cuique opera sua, vel bona vel mala, cuncta in memoriam revocentur et mentis intuitu mira celeritate cernantur ut accuset vel excuset scientia conscientiam atque ita simul et omnes et singuli iudicentur. Quae nimirum vis divina libri nomen accepit. In ea quippe quodam modo legitur quidquid ea faciente recolitur.*

31   CD 20.15: *Non Deum liber iste commemorat ne oblivione fallatur; sed praedestinationem significat eorum quibus aeterna dabitur vita.*

Neque enim nescit eos Deus et in hoc libro legit, ut sciat; sed potius
ipsa eius praescientia de illis, quae falli non potest, liber est vitae, in
quo sunt scripti, id est ante praecogniti.

32   CD 21.24: *Nunc enim propterea pro eis orat quos in genere humano*
habet inimicos quia tempus est paenitentiae fructuosae. Nam quid
maxime pro eis orat, nisi "ut det illis Deus," sicut dicit apostolus,
"paenitentiam et resipiscant de diaboli laqueis, a quo captivi
tenentur secundum ipsius voluntatem?" Denique si de aliquibus
ita certa esset, ut qui sint illi etiam nosset qui, licet adhuc in hac
vita sint constituti, tamen praedestinati sunt in aeternum ignem ire
cum diabolo, tam pro eis non oraret quam nec pro ipso. Sed quia
de nullo certa est, orat pro omnibus dumtaxat hominibus inimicis
suis in hoc corpore constitutis, nec tamen pro omnibus exauditur.
Pro his enim solis exauditur qui, etsi adversantur ecclesiae, ita sunt
tamen praedestinati ut pro eis exaudiatur ecclesia et filii efficiantur
ecclesiae.

33   CD 17.4: *quoniam non iudicabuntur quae in melius vel in deterius*
medio tempore commutantur, sed in quibus extremis inventus fuerit
qui iudicabitur. Propter quod dictum est: "Qui perseveraverit usque
in finem, hic salvus erit."

Chapter 4

1   CD 13.11: *Ita etiam in transcursu temporum quaeritur praesens, nec*
inuenitur.

2   CF 9.10.24: *cumque ad eum finem sermo perduceretur, ut carnalium*
sensuum delectatio quantalibet, in quantalibet luce corporea, prae
illius vitae iucunditate non comparatione sed ne commemoratione
quidem digna videretur, erigentes nos ardentiore affectu in idipsum,
perambulavimus gradatim cuncta corporalia et ipsum caelum, unde
sol et luna et stellae lucent super terram. et adhuc ascendebamus
interius cogitando et loquendo et mirando opera tua. et venimus
in mentes nostras et transcendimus eas, ut attingeremus regionem
ubertatis indeficientis, ubi pascis Israhel in aeternum veritate pabulo,
et ibi vita sapientia est […].

3   CF 9.10.24: *[…], per quam fiunt omnia ista, et quae fuerunt et*
quae futura sunt, et ipsa non fit, sed sic est ut fuit, et sic erit semper.
quin potius fuisse et futurum esse non est in ea, sed esse solum,
quoniam aeterna est: nam fuisse et futurum esse non est aeternum.
et dum loquimur et inhiamus illi, attingimus eam modice toto ictu
cordis. et suspiravimus et reliquimus ibi religatas primitias spiritus
et remeavimus ad strepitum oris nostri, ubi verbum et incipitur et

finitur. et quid simile verbo tuo, domino nostro, in se permanenti sine vetustate atque innovanti omnia?

Chapter 5

1   CF 8.1.1: *nec certior de te sed stabilior in te esse cupiebam. de mea vero temporali vita nutabant omnia et mundandum erat cor a fermento veteri.*
2   CF 8.2.4: *ergo parietes faciunt christianos?*
3   CF 8.3.8: *ubique maius gaudium molestia maiore praeceditur. quid est hoc, domine deus meus, cum tu aeternum tibi, tu ipse, sis gaudium, et quaedam de te circa te semper gaudeant? quid est quod haec rerum pars alternat defectu et profectu, offensionibus et conciliationibus? an is est modus earum et tantum dedisti eis, cum a summis caelorum usque ad ima terrarum, ab initio usque in finem saeculorum, ab angelo usque ad vermiculum, a motu primo usque ad extremum, omnia genera bonorum et omnia iusta opera tua suis quaeque sedibus locares et suis quaeque temporibus ageres?*
4   CF 8.5.10: *ligatus non ferro alieno sed mea ferrea voluntate. velle meum tenebat inimicus et inde mihi catenam fecerat et constrinxerat me. quippe ex voluntate perversa facta est libido, et dum servitur libidini, facta est consuetudo, et dum consuetudini non resistitur, facta est necessitas. quibus quasi ansulis sibimet innexis (unde catenam appellavi) tenebat me obstrictum dura servitus. voluntas autem nova quae mihi esse coeperat, ut te gratis colerem fruique te vellem, deus, sola certa iucunditas, nondum erat idonea ad superandam priorem vetustate roboratam. ita duae voluntates meae, una vetus, alia nova, illa carnalis, illa spiritalis, confligebant inter se atque discordando dissipabant animam meam.*
5   CF 8.5.12: *non enim erat quod tibi responderem dicenti mihi, "surge qui dormis et exsurge a mortuis, et inluminabit te Christus," et undique ostendenti vera te dicere, non erat omnino quid responderem veritate convictus, nisi tantum verba lenta et somnolenta: "modo," "ecce modo," "sine paululum." sed "modo et modo" non habebat modum et "sine paululum" in longum ibat.*
6   CF 8.6.15: *amicus autem dei, si voluero, ecce nunc fio.*
7   CF 8.6.15: *namque dum legit et volvit fluctus cordis sui, infremuit aliquando et discrevit decrevitque meliora, iamque tuus ait amico suo, ego iam abrupi me ab illa spe nostra et deo servire statui, et hoc ex hac hora, in hoc loco aggredior.*
8   CF 8.7.17: *differebam contempta felicitate terrena ad eam investigandam vacare.*

9   CF 8.7.17: *at ego adulescens miser valde, miser in exordio ipsius adulescentiae, etiam petieram a te castitatem et dixeram, "da mihi castitatem et continentiam, sed noli modo."*

10   CF 8.7.18: *et putaveram me propterea differre de die in diem contempta spe saeculi te solum sequi, quia non mihi apparebat certum aliquid quo dirigerem cursum meum. et venerat dies quo nudarer mihi.*

11   CF 8.8.20: *tam multa ergo feci, ubi non hoc erat velle quod posse: et non faciebam quod et incomparabili affectu amplius mihi placebat, et mox ut vellem possem, quia mox ut vellem, utique vellem. ibi enim facultas ea, quae voluntas, et ipsum velle iam facere erat; et tamen non fiebat.*

12   CF 8.10.22: *ego cum deliberabam ut iam servirem domino deo meo, sicut diu disposueram, ego eram qui volebam, ego qui nolebam: ego eram. nec plene volebam nec plene nolebam. ideo mecum contendebam et dissipabar a me ipso, et ipsa dissipatio me invito quidem fiebat, nec tamen ostendebat naturam mentis alienae sed poenam meae. et ideo non iam ego operabar illam.*

13   CF 8.10.24: *si omnia concurrant in unum articulum temporis pariterque cupiantur omnia quae simul agi nequeunt, discerpunt enim animum sibimet adversantibus quattuor voluntatibus vel etiam pluribus in tanta copia rerum quae appetuntur.*

14   CF 8.10.24: *nam quaero ab eis utrum bonum sit delectari lectione apostoli et utrum bonum sit delectari psalmo sobrio et utrum bonum sit evangelium disserere. respondebunt ad singula: "bonum." quid si ergo pariter delectent omnia simulque uno tempore, nonne diversae voluntates distendunt cor hominis, dum deliberatur quid potissimum arripiamus? et omnes bonae sunt et certant secum, donec eligatur unum quo feratur tota voluntas una, quae in plures dividebatur.*

15   CF 8.11.25: *dicebam enim apud me intus, "ecce modo fiat, modo fiat," et cum verbo iam ibam in placitum. iam paene faciebam et non faciebam ... et paulo minus ibi eram et paulo minus, iam iamque attingebam et tenebam. et non ibi eram nec attingebam nec tenebam.*

16   CF 8.11.25: *punctumque ipsum temporis quo aliud futurus eram, quanto propius admovebatur, tanto ampliorem incutiebat horrorem. sed non recutiebat retro nec avertebat, sed suspendebat.*

17   CF 8.11.27: *tardabant tamen cunctantem me ...*

18   CF 8.11.27: *ista controversia in corde meo non nisi de me ipso adversus me ipsum.*

19   CF 8.12.29: *statim quippe cum fine huiusce sententiae quasi luce securitatis infusa cordi meo omnes dubitationis tenebrae diffugerunt.*

20   DP 1.1: *Asserimus ergo donum Dei esse perseverantiam qua usque in finem perseveratur in Christo. Finem autem dico, quo vita ista finitur, in qua tantummodo periculum est ne cadatur. Itaque utrum quisque*

hoc munus acceperit, quamdiu hanc vitam ducit, incertum est. Si enim priusquam moriatur cadat, non perseverasse utique dicitur, et verissime dicitur.

21   DP 5.8: *Praeterita enim sunt peccata, quae nobis ut dimittantur oramus: perseverantia vero quae in aeternum salvos facit, tempori quidem hujus vitae, non tamen peracto, sed ei quod usque ad ejus finem restat, est necessaria.*

22   DP 5.10: *quae si data est, perseveratum est usque in finem; si autem non est perseveratum usque in finem, non est data. […] Non itaque dicant homines, perseverantiam cuiquam datam usque in finem, nisi cum ipse venerit finis, et perseverasse, cui data est, repertus fuerit usque in finem.*

23   DP 24.66: *Quod donum qui non habet […] alia quaecumque habet, inaniter habet.*

24   DP 8.19: *Hominibus autem videtur, omnes qui boni apparent fideles, perseverantiam usque in finem accipere debuisse. Deus autem melius esse judicavit, miscere quosdam non perseveraturos certo numero sanctorum suorum; ut quibus non expedit in hujus vitae tentatione securitas, non possint esse securi. Multos enim a perniciosa elatione reprimit quod ait Apostolus: "Quapropter, qui videtur stare, videat ne cadat."*

25   DP 13.32: *ipsosque regeneratos, alios perseverantes usque in finem hinc ire, alios quousque decidant hic teneri.*

26   DP 15.38: *Fuit quidam in nostro monasterio, qui corripientibus fratribus cur quaedam non facienda faceret, et facienda non faceret, respondebat: "Qualiscumque nunc sim, talis ero qualem me Deus futurum esse praescivit." Qui profecto et verum dicebat, et hoc vero non proficiebat in bonum: sed usque adeo profecit in malum, ut deserta monasterii societate fieret canis reversus ad suum vomitum: et tamen adhuc qualis sit futurus, incertum est.*

27   DP 7.13: *Post casum autem hominis, nonnisi ad gratiam suam Deus voluit pertinere, ut homo accedat ad eum; neque nisi ad gratiam suam voluit pertinere, ut homo non recedat ab eo.*

28   DP 5.12: *Nihil enim fit, nisi quod aut ipse facit, aut fieri ipse permittit. Potens ergo est, et a malo in bonum flectere voluntates, et in lapsum pronas convertere, ac dirigere in sibi placitum gressum. Cui non frustra dicitur, "Deus, tu convertens vivificabis nos."*

29   DP 8.19: *In cogitatione autem sua vel cadit quisque, vel stat.*

30   DP 8.19: *beatus Ambrosius audet et dicit: "Non enim in potestate nostra cor nostrum, et nostrae cogitationes." Quod omnis qui humiliter et veraciter pius est, esse verissimum sentit.*

31   DP 8.20, quoting the first chapter of Ambrose's *De Fuga Saeculi*: *Non enim in potestate nostra cor nostrum et cogitationes nostrae,*

*quae improviso offusae mentem animumque confundunt, atque
alio trahunt quam tu proposueris: ad saecularia revocant,
mundana inserunt, voluptuaria ingerunt, illecebrosa intexunt,
ipsoque in tempore quo elevare mentem paramus, inserti inanibus
cogitationibus ad terrena plerumque dejicimur.*

32 DP 19.49: *a Deo enim praeparatur voluntas hominum.*

33 DP 22.60: *et volentes ex nolentibus faciat.*

34 DP 23.64: *Ubi intelligimus, et hoc ipsum esse donum Dei, ut veraci
corde et spiritualiter clamemus ad Deum. Attendant ergo quomodo
falluntur, qui putant esse a nobis, non dari nobis, ut petamus,
quaeramus, pulsemus: et hoc esse dicunt, quod gratia praeceditur
merito nostro, ut sequatur illa, cum accipimus petentes, et invenimus
quaerentes, aperiturque pulsantibus: nec volunt intelligere etiam hoc
divini muneris esse, ut oremus, hoc est, petamus, quaeramus, atque
pulsemus.*

35 DP 22.62: *exsultate ei cum tremore: quoniam de vita aeterna, quam
filiis promissionis promisit non mendax Deus ante tempora aeterna,
nemo potest esse securus, nisi consummata fuerit ista vita, quae
tentatio est super terram.*

36 DP 20.53: *Et in eisdem etiam libris quod de mea conversione
narravi, Deo me convertente ad eam fidem, quam miserrima
et furiosissima loquacitate vastabam, nonne ita narratum esse
meministis, ut ostenderem me fidelibus et quotidianis matris meae
lacrymis ne perirem fuisse concessum.*

37 DP 20.53: *De proficiente porro perseverantia quemadmodum Deum
rogaverim.*

Chapter 6

1 CD 17.20: *"Vae tibi, terra,"* inquit, *"cuius rex adulescens, et
principes tui mane comedunt. Beata tu, terra, cuius rex tuus filius
ingenuorum, et principes tui in tempore comedunt, in fortitudine, et
non in confusione."*

2 CD 17.20: *Principes illius civitatis mane manducantes, id est ante
horam congruam, quia non expectant oportunam quae vera est in
futuro saeculo felicitatem, festinanter beari huius saeculi celebritate
cupientes; principes autem civitatis Christi tempus non fallacis
beatitudinis patienter expectant.*

REFERENCES

Agamben, Giorgio. 2005. *The Time That Remains: A Commentary on the Letter to the Romans*. Translated by Patricia Daley. Stanford: Stanford University Press.

Agamben, Giorgio. 2007. *Infancy and History: The Destruction of Experience*. Translated by Liz Heron. New York: Verso.

Agamben, Giorgio. 2013. *The Highest Poverty: Monastic Rules and Form-of-Life*. Stanford: Stanford University Press.

Aristotle. 1929–34. *Physics*. Translated by P.H. Wicksteed and F.M. Cornford. Cambridge, MA: Harvard University Press.

Augustine. 1865. *De Dono Perseverantiae*. Patrologia Latina 45, 933–1004. Paris: Migne.

Augustine. 1955a. *De Civitate Dei*. CCSL 47–8. Edited by B. Dombart and A. Kalb. Turnhout: Brepols.

Augustine. 1955b. *Homilies on 1 John*. In *Later Works*. Translated by John Burnaby. Philadelphia: Westminster.

Augustine. 1969. *De Catechizandis Rudibus*. CCSL 46. Edited by J.-B. Bauer. Turnhout: Brepols.

Augustine. 1981. *Confessiones*. CCSL 27. Edited by Luc Verheijen. Turnhout: Brepols.

Augustine. 1992. *Sermons (94a–147a): On the New Testament*. III.4. Translated by Edmund Hill, O.P. Brooklyn NY: New City.

Augustine. 2002. *The Literal Meaning of Genesis*. Translated by Edmund Hill, O.P. Hyde Park, NY: New City.

Baker-Brian, Nicholas J. 2011. *Manichaeism: An Ancient Faith Rediscovered*. London: T&T Clark.

BeDuhn, Jason. 2000. *The Manichaean Body in Discipline and Ritual*. Baltimore: Johns Hopkins University Press.

BeDuhn, Jason. 2009. *Augustine's Manichaean Dilemma, Volume 1: Conversion and Apostasy, 373–388 CE*. Philadelphia: University of Pennsylvania Press

BeDuhn, Jason. 2013. *Augustine's Manichaean Dilemma, Volume 2: Making a "Catholic" Self, 388–401 CE*. Philadelphia: University of Pennsylvania Press.

Belfield, Jane. 1978. *Tarlton's News Out of Purgatory (1590): A Modern-Spelling Edition, with Introduction and Commentary*. Dissertation submitted to the Shakespeare Institute at the University of Birmingham.

Benjamin, Walter. 2007. *Illuminations: Essays and Reflections*. Translated by Harry Zohn. New York: Schocken.

Bennington, Geoffrey. 2011. "A Moment of Madness: Derrida's Kierkegaard." *Oxford Literary Review* 33, no. 1: 103–27.

Bilger, Burkhard. 2011. "The Possibilian." *New Yorker*, April 25. Online: https://www.newyorker.com/magazine/2011/04/25/the-possibilian (accessed May 1, 2019).

Boersma, Gerald. 2017. "Augustine's Immanent Critique of Stoicism." *Scottish Journal of Theology* 70, no. 2 (May): 184–97.

Burrus, Virginia. 1999. "An Immoderate Feast: Augustine Reads John's Apocalypse." *Augustinian Studies* 30, no. 2: 183–94.

Byers, Sarah. 2007. "Augustine on the 'Divided Self': Platonist or Stoic?" *Augustinian Studies* 38, no. 1: 105–18.

Byers, Sarah. 2013. *Perception, Sensibility, and Moral Motivation in Augustine: A Stoic-Platonic Synthesis*. Cambridge: Cambridge University Press.

Casiday, A. M. C. 2005. "Grace and the Humanity of Christ According to St. Vincent of Lérins." *Vigiliae Christianae* 59, no. 3: 298–314.

Cavadini, John. 2007. "The Darkest Enigma: Reconsidering the Self in Augustine's Thought." *Augustinian Studies* 38, no. 1: 119–32.

Christensen, Jen 2017. "Meaningful Mindfulness: How It Could Help You Be Happier, Healthier, and More Successful." *CNN*, February 15. Online: https://www.cnn.com/2017/02/15/health/mindfulness-meditation-techniques/ (accessed November 5, 2018).

Collier, Andrew. 2001. *Christianity and Marxism: A Philosophical Contribution to Their Reconciliation*. London: Routledge.

Dassmann, Ernst. 1996. "*Fuga Saeculi*: Aspekte frühchristlicher Kulturkritik bei Ambrosius und Augustinus." In *Wege der Theologie: An der Schwelle zum dritten Jahrtausend*, edited by Günter Risse, Heino Sonnemans, and Burkhard Thess, 939–950. Paderborn: Bonifatius.

Davenport, Guy. 1981. *Herakleitos and Diogenes*. San Francisco: Grey Fox.

DeLanda, Manuel, and Graham Harman. 2017. *The Rise of Realism*. Cambridge: Polity.

Derrida, Jacques. 1978. "*Cogito* and the History of Madness." In *Writing and Difference*. Translated by Alan Bass, 31–63. Chicago: University of Chicago Press.

Derrida, Jacques. 1992. *Given Time: Counterfeit Money, Volume 1*. Translated by Peggy Kamuf. Chicago: University of Chicago Press.

Dreyfus, Georges. 2011. "Is Mindfulness Present-Centred and Non-Judgmental?" *Contemporary Buddhism* 12, no. 1: 41–54.

Epictetus. 2014. *Discourses, Fragments, Handbook*. Translated by Robin Hard. Oxford: Oxford University Press.

Farrell, John. 2005. *The Day Without Yesterday: Lemaître, Einstein, and the Birth of Modern Cosmology*. New York: Avalon.

Forbes, David. 2019. "How Capitalism Captured the Mindfulness Industry." *The Guardian*, April 16. Online: https://www.theguardian.com/lifeandstyle/2019/apr/16/how-capitalism-captured-the-mindfulness-industry (accessed October 15, 2019).

Frend, W. H. C. 1989. "Augustine and Orosius: On the End of the Ancient World." *Augustinian Studies* 20: 1–38.

Gilson, Etienne. 1960. *The Christian Philosophy of Saint Augustine*. Translated by L. E. M. Lynch. New York: Octagon.

Gratton, Peter. 2013. "Post-Deconstructive Realism: It's About Time." *Speculations* 4: 84–90.

Gundersdorf von Jess, Wilma. 1972. "Augustine: A Consistent and Unitary Theory of Time." *New Scholasticism* 46: 337–51.

Hadot, Pierre. 2001. *The Inner Citadel: The Meditations of Marcus Aurelius*. Translated by Michael Chase. Cambridge, MA: Harvard University Press.

Hadot, Pierre. 2009. *The Present Alone Is Our Happiness*. Edited by Jeannie Cartier and Arnold I. Davidson. Stanford: Stanford University Press.

Hägglund, Martin. 2019. *This Life: Secular Faith and Spiritual Freedom*. New York: Pantheon.

Hannan, Sean. 2019. "Augustine's Time of Death in *City of God* 13." *Augustinian Studies* 50, no. 1: 43–63.

Harman, Graham. 2005. *Guerrilla Metaphysics: Phenomenology and the Carpentry of Things*. Chicago: Open Court.

Harman, Graham. 2011. "The Road to Objects." *Continent* 1, no. 3: 171–9.

Heidegger, Martin. 1962. *Being and Time*. Translated by John MacQuarrie and Edward Robinson. San Francisco: Harper & Row.

Humphries, Thomas. 2009. "Distentio Animi: Praesens Temporis, Imago Aeternitatis." *Augustinian Studies* 40, no. 1: 75–101.

Jordan, Robert. 1955. "Time and Contingency in St. Augustine." *Review of Metaphysics* 8: 394–417.

Kaufman, Peter Iver. 2003. "Patience and/or Politics: Augustine and the Crisis at Calama, 408–409." *Vigiliae Christianae* 57, no. 1: 22–35.

King, Jr., Martin Luther. 2013. "Letter from Birmingham Jail." In Jonathan Rieder, *Gospel of Freedom: Martin Luther King, Jr.'s Letter from Birmingham Jail and the Struggle that Changed a Nation*, 169–86. New York: Bloomsbury.

Lacey, Hugh M. 1968. "Empiricism and Augustine's Problems about Time." *Review of Metaphysics* 22: 219–45.

Lambert, Dominique. 2000. *Un Atome d'Univers: La vie et l'œuvre de Georges Lemaître*. Brussels: Lessius.

Langer, Ellen. 2017. *Mindfulness*. Boston: Harvard Business Review Press.

Lee, Gregory W. 2016. "Using the Earthly City: Ecclesiology, Political Activity, and Religious Coercion in Augustine." *Augustinian Studies* 47, no. 1: 41–63.

Lemaître, Georges. 1950. *The Primeval Atom: An Essay on Cosmogony*. Translated by Betty H. and Serge A. Korff. New York: Van Nostrand.

Long, A. A. 2002. *Epictetus: A Stoic and Socratic Guide to Life*. Oxford: Oxford University Press.

Löwith, Karl. 1949. *Meaning in History*. Chicago: University of Chicago Press.

Malcolm X. 1965. *Malcolm X Speaks*. Edited by George Breitman. New York: Merit.

Marcus Aurelius. 1916. *Mediations*. Translated by C.R. Haines. Cambridge, MA: Harvard University Press.

Marion, Jean-Luc. 2012. *In the Self's Place: The Approach of Saint Augustine*. Translated by Jeffrey L. Kosky. Stanford: Stanford University Press.

Markus, R. A. 1967. "Marius Victorinus and Augustine." In *The Cambridge History of Late Greek and Early Medieval Philosophy*, edited by A.H. Armstrong, 402–5. Cambridge: Cambridge University Press.

Markus, R. A. 1989. *Saeculum: History and Society in the Theology of Saint Augustine*. Cambridge: Cambridge University Press.

Marrou, Henri-Irénée. 1950. *L'Ambivalence du Temps de l'Histoire chez Augustin*. Montreal: Institut d'Études Médiévales.

McCabe, Herbert. 1980. "Class Struggle and Christian Love." In *Agenda for Prophets: Toward a Political Theology for Britain*, edited by David Haslam and Rex Ambler, 153–69. London: Bowerdean.

McLynn, Neil B. 1999. "Augustine's Roman Empire." *Augustinian Studies* 30, no. 2: 29–44.

McTaggart, John. 1908. "The Unreality of Time." *Mind* 17: 457–74.

Mendelson, Michael. 2000. "*Venter Animi/Distentio Animi*: Memory and Temporality in Augustine's *Confessions*." *Augustinian Studies* 31, no. 2: 137–63.

Miner, Robert. 2007. "Augustinian Recollection." *Augustinian Studies* 38, no. 2: 435–50.

Modern Stoicism. Online: https://modernstoicism.com/about-stoic-week/ (accessed July 14, 2019).

Morrison, Toni. 1996. "The Future of Time: Literature and Diminished Expectations." 25th Jefferson Lecture in the Humanities. National

Endowment of the Humanities. Washington D.C. March 25, 1996. Online: https://neh.dspacedirect.org/handle/11215/3774 (accessed July 15, 2019).

Ogliari, Donato. 2003. *Gratia et Certamen: The Relationship Between Grace and Free Will in the Discussion of Augustine with the So-Called Semipelagians*. Leuven: Peeters.

O'Loughlin, Thomas. 1999. "The Development of Augustine the Bishop's Critique of Astrology." *Augustinian Studies* 30, no. 1: 83–103.

Ostriker, Jeremiah P., and Simon Mitton. 2013. *Heart of Darkness: Unraveling the Mysteries of the Invisible Universe*. Princeton: Princeton University Press.

Pinker, Steven. 2018. *Enlightenment Now: The Case for Reason, Science, Humanism, and Progress*. New York: Viking.

Plato. 1926. *Parmenides*. Translated by Harold North Fowler. Cambridge, MA: Harvard University Press.

Plato. 1929. *Timaeus*. Translated by R. G. Bury. Cambridge, MA: Harvard University Press.

Plotinus. 1967. *Enneads*. Translated by A. H. Armstrong. Cambridge, MA: Harvard University Press.

Pranger, M. B. 2010. *Eternity's Ennui: Temporality, Perseverance, and Voice in Augustine and Western Literature*. Leiden: Brill.

Quinn, John M. 1992. "Four Faces of Time in Augustine." *Recherches Augustiniennes* 26: 181–231.

Rogers, Katherin A. 1994. "Eternity Has No Duration." *Religious Studies* 30: 1–16.

Rogers, Katherin A. 1996. "St. Augustine on Time and Eternity." *American Catholic Philosophical Quarterly* 70, no. 2: 207–23.

Ross, Donald L. 1991. "Time, the Heaven of Heavens, and Memory in Augustine's *Confessions*." *Augustinian Studies* 22: 191–205.

Russell, Bertrand. 1948. *Human Knowledge: Its Scope and Limits*. New York: Simon & Schuster.

Sears, Richard W. 2014. *Mindfulness: Living Through Challenges and Enriching Your Life in This Moment*. Hoboken, NJ: Wiley-Blackwell.

Shaviro, Steven. 2011. "The Actual Volcano: Whitehead, Harman, and the Problem of Relations." In *The Speculative Turn: Continental Materialism and Realism*, edited by Levi Bryant, Graham Harman, and Nick Srnicek, 272–90. Melbourne: Re.Press.

Sorabji, Richard. 1983. *Time, Creation, and Continuum: Theories in Antiquity and the Early Middle Ages*. Ithaca, NY: Cornell University Press.

Sorabji, Richard. 2005. *The Philosophy of the Commentators, 200-600 AD*. Vol. II. Ithaca, NY: Cornell University Press.

Strozynski, Mateusz. 2009. "Time, Self, and Aporia: Spiritual Exercise in Saint Augustine." *Augustinian Studies* 40, no. 1: 103–20.

Teske, Roland. 1983. "The World-Soul and Time in St. Augustine." *Augustinian Studies* 14: 75–92.

Teske, Roland. 1996. *Paradoxes of Time in St. Augustine*. Milwaukee, WI: Marquette University Press.

Ticciati, Susannah. 2010. "Augustine and Grace Ex Nihilo: The Logic of Augustine's Response to the Monks of Hadrumetum and Marseilles." *Augustinian Studies* 41, no. 2: 401–22.

Van Dusen, David. 2014. *The Space of Time: A Sensualist Interpretation of Time in Augustine, Confessions X to XII*. Leiden: Brill.

Warren, James. 2002. *Epicurus and Democritean Ethics: An Archaeology of Ataraxia*. Cambridge: Cambridge University Press

Wetzel, James. 1992. *Augustine and the Limits of Virtue*. Cambridge: Cambridge University Press.

Whippman, Ruth. 2016. "Actually, Let's Not Be in the Moment." *New York Times*, November 26. Online: https://www.nytimes.com/2016/11/26/opinion/sunday/actually-lets-not-be-in-the-moment.html (accessed September 15, 2018).

Williams, Mark, and Danny Penman. 2011. *Mindfulness: An Eight-Week Plan for Finding Peace in a Frantic World*. New York: Rodale.

Wood, James. 2019. "If God Is Dead, Your Time Is Everything." *New Yorker*, May 20. Online: https://www.newyorker.com/magazine/2019/05/20/if-god-is-dead-your-time-is-everything (accessed June 1, 2019).

Wyschogrod, Edith. 1990. *Saints and Postmodernism: Revisioning Moral Philosophy*. Chicago: University of Chicago Press.

INDEX

www.ingramcontent.com/pod-product-compliance
Ingram Content Group UK Ltd.
Pitfield, Milton Keynes, MK11 3LW, UK
UKHW031251020325
455690UK00007B/102